The Living Art of
BONSAI

The Living Art of
BONSAI

Principles & Techniques of Cultivation & Propagation

Professor Amy Liang

Sterling Publishing Co., Inc.   New York

Publisher: Dixson D. S. Sung
Consultant: Lee Kuo-an
Art Director: Liang Cheng-chu
Executive Editor: Bobby N. C. Chang
Photographers: Lin Shih-tse, Tao Hsuan-hsi, Chao Tien-teh,
              Kao Chih-tsun, Sun Hsien-jung,
              Liang Cheng-chu, Fuh King-fwu
Assistant Photographers: Chuang Chung-hsien, Chen Tien-shou
Artistic Editors: Liang Cheng-chu, Lu Ta-kuan, Jade Hsieh
Literary Editors: Crystal Wang, Wang Sheng-ying,
              Bobby N. C. Chang

Library of Congress Cataloging-in-Publication Data Available

10   9   8   7   6   5   4   3

First paperback edition published in 1995 by
Sterling Publishing Company, Inc.
387 Park Avenue South, New York, N.Y. 10016
Originally published and © 1991 by Hilit Publishing Company, Ltd.
Distributed in Canada by Sterling Publishing
℅ Canadian Manda Group, One Atlantic Avenue, Suite 105
Toronto, Ontario, Canada M6K 3E7
Distributed in Great Britain and Europe by Cassell PLC
Villiers House, 41/47 Strand, London WC2N 5JE, England
Printed and bound in Hong Kong
All rights reserved

Sterling ISBN 0-8069-8780-4 Trade
            0-8069-8781-2 Paper

Dedication to my father, Liang Wan-hsing, and my mother, Liang-Lin Yen

Thank you for bringing me into the world, giving me instruction and education, and raising me with your endless love. You led me to overcome the challenges of darkness, sorrow and sickness and you taught me how to await the coming of peace and hope. I will dedicate this book to you and say, ''I'll love you forever.''

To the memory of

Marvine Burke and Hsu Feng-ho

Thank you for your love and encouragement. Though the publication of this book was delayed, I have kept my word to dedicate this book to you in front of your tombs. Both of you will be always on my mind.

Many thanks to

My husband, Dr. Chang Han-tung, and my family

All of you are the greatest, kindest, and the most reliable persons to me. Without your love, patience, and encouragement, I could not devote myself to bonsai cultivation and writing. I want to tell you that nobody in the world could be as kind to me as you are.

My teacher, Hsu Chien-tien, and Dr. Su Wu-hsiung

Thank you for saving my life from the devil of illness himself and encouraging me to recover from the blow with the natural essence of bonsai cultivation. My existence and achievement wouldn't have been true without your help.

Lee Kuo-an

Thank you for giving me so many valuable opinions and suggestions. Without your help, the book could not have been produced so easily.

Contents

Preface by the President of Seattle Pacific University

The ancient art of bonsai is truly a fine art in the academic sense. With its cultural heritage imbedded in China, the art of bonsai continues to inspire awe and beauty in those who have come to know it.

We at Seattle Pacific University have been privileged to have Professor Amy Chang-Liang share her mastery of the art of bonsai in a course at the School of Fine and Performing Arts.

With her dedication to teaching the art of bonsai, she has stimulated the enthusiasm for bonsai of many students and bonsai lovers at our university. Many associations of bonsai and several universities in different countries have extended invitations to her to give lectures on bonsai, and her lectures and demonstrations have attracted numerous audiences. We are very proud to have such an excellent professor at our university.

Professor Amy Chang-Liang is a consummate representative of the art of bonsai to all who desire to understand or get involved. In addition to teaching the techniques of bonsai, Professor Amy Chang-Liang provides both an historical and philosophical grounding in the art. This volume is useful both to the beginner and advanced artist of bonsai.

Dr. David C. Le Shana
President
S.P.U. Seattle Pacific University

Chinese Publisher's Preface

To many people, bonsai is just a Japanese thing. In fact, the art of bonsai originated in China. The word itself first made an appearance during the Chin dynasty, when landscape literature and the art of gardening began to gain popularity.

The Chinese respect nature and love to enjoy the beauty of mountains and rivers to help clean away worries. To gain the company of nature in their homes they bring mountains and trees indoors and plant them in a pot, demonstrating the truth of the saying: "The world can exist in a grain of sand and the universe in a leaf." This was the original spirit of bonsai, to respect and embrace nature. It is an art derived from nature, but built on the close relationship between human beings and nature.

"Bonsai" is a commonly used word throughout the world. It comes from the Japanese pronunciation of the Chinese word "pen-tsai." From the universal use of this Japanese word, we can see how great the Japanese influence has been upon the art. Today the Chinese use the term "pen-ching" and many enthusiastic bonsai growers are trying to discover more about the many different styles of traditional schools from ancient scriptures and records and to combine their discoveries with the essence of Japanese achievements in cultivation. Thus, a new art of bonsai is developing that belongs to modern Chinese culture.

We at Hilit Publishing respect the efforts of the modern bonsai enthusiasts to promote and develop this traditional art. To show our support, dozens of our photographers, artists, and editors have cooperated with the author, Professor Amy Liang, over a long period of time to present all aspects of bonsai of every season and help the development of the legacy of Chinese bonsai.

Dixson D. S. Sung
President
Hilit Publishing Co., Ltd.

Author's Preface

Bonsai is an essential part of Chinese culture which has flourished thousands of years. It is also the crystallization of both the Chinese aesthetic life style and the art of gardening.

"There is a world in a stone and a view in a tree." I have devoted myself to bonsai cultivation for 20 years. My experience with bonsai reveals that a bonsai lover can obtain a lot of lessons and inspiration from contact with bonsai every day even though plants cannot speak themselves. We can apply the spirit and the essence of plants and rocks to train bonsai in pots. Using our imagination, we can apply creative techniques to enjoy the fun of bonsai and the beauty of nature. At the same time, we forget our worries and tensions and feel peaceful in our minds. I did not expect the pleasure of bonsai would be so great when I started to grow bonsai during rehabilitation a long time ago, but now I want to let everyone share the wonder and joy of it.

I have drawn upon all my lectures to schools and clubs, upon my records and experience and on materials from "The Art of Chinese Bonsai in Taiwan" TV series, to write this book— "The Living Art of Bonsai." The purpose of this book is to provide bonsai beginners and other bonsai lovers with correct cultivating methods and techniques. It is also a reference book for bonsai creation. I hope Chinese people who are proud of our profound culture in the East can work together to promote the essence of our culture— bonsai — and make it a common art that will become part of our lives. Hopefully, in the near future, everyone will be proud of having bonsai at home.

All the materials, decorations, stands, pots, and bonsai illustrated in the book are from my collection. Please do not worry about the unfinished bonsai in some pictures. Since bonsai is a living art, I am sure they will grow well with care and the passage of time.

I would like to give my blessing to all the readers. May the lively and wonderful bonsai offer you a healthy and happy life, while introducing you to one of the infinite pleasures in life.

July 7, 1988
Amy Liang
at Purple Yard, Teng Mou, Taipei

紫園

七十年辛酉
之八月十八日
八十三叟大千張爰

A congratulatory message in Chinese calligraphy dedicated to the author by the famous calligrapher Chang Ta-ch'ien.

BONSAI APPRECIATION

Trident maple/*Acer burergerianum* Miq. Height: 29 in.
(An Entry displayed at the 63rd Kokufu Bonsai Exhibition in Tokyo, Japan.)

Trident maple (front view of the bonsai on page 14 in leafless phase).

Trident maple (rear view of the bonsai above).

Formosan hackberry/*Celtis formosana* Hayata. Height: 14 in.
(A bonsai chosen as a model for the R.O.C. stamps below.)

Formosan hackberry (same bonsai on page 16 in leafless phase).

Common jasmin orange/*Murraya paniculata* Jack. Height: 36 in.

Chinese hackberry/*Celtis sinensis* Pers. Forest-style group planting. Height: 29 in.
(A bonsai chosen as a model for the R.O.C. stamp above.)

Box-tree/
Buxus harlandii
Hance in Journ.
Spring appearance.
Height: 19 in.

Box-tree (autumn appearance of the bonsai above).

Seven Star Mountain (ch'i-hsing-shan) azalea/
Rhododendron nakaharai Hayata in bloom. Height: 26 in.

Sargent juniper/*Juniperus chinensis* L. *var. Sargenti* Henry. Height: 19 in.

Sargent juniper (same bonsai on page 22).
An entry displayed at the 65th Kokufu Bonsai Exhibition in Tokyo, Japan.

Formosan hackberry/*Celtis formosana* Hayata. Height: 34 in.
(An entry displayed at the 1989 Worldwide Bonsai Exhibition.)

Formosan hackberry (same bonsai on page 24 in leafless phase).

Box-tree/*Buxus harlandii* Hance in Journ. Height: 34 in.
(A bonsai chosen as a model for the R.O.C. stamp above.)

Satsuki azalea ''Kogetsu''/*Rhododendron indicum* Sweet in bloom. Height: 36 in.

Japanese gray-bark elm (zelkova)/*Zelkova serrata* Makino in forest-style group planting. Height: 34 in.

Japanese gray-bark elm (same bonsai on page 28 in leafless phase).

Chinese elm/*Ulmus parvifolia* Jacq. Height: 35 in.

Chinese elm (same bonsai on page 30 in leafless phase).

Flowering apricot/*Prunus mume* Sieb. et Zucc. Height: 36 in.

Flowering apricot (same bonsai on page 32 in leafless phase)

Satsuki azalea ''Kinsai''/*Rhododendron indicum* Sweet in bloom. Height: 28 in.

Japanese premna/*Premna microphylla* Turcz. Height: 40 in.

Needle juniper/*Juniperus rigida* Sieb. et Zucc. Height: 24 in.
(Selected as an entry in the 58th Aifu Bonsai Exhibition.)

Flowering apricot/*Prunus mume* Sieb. et Zucc. Height: 35 in.

Sargent juniper/*Juniperus chinensis* L. *var. Sargenti* Henry. Height: 34 in.
(On display at the U.S. Pacific Bonsai Museum.)

Japanese wisteria/*Wisteria floribunda* DC. Height: 19 in.

Japanese red maple ''Chishio''/*Acer formosum* Carr.
Height: 12 in.

Japanese gray-bark elm
(zelkova)/*Zelkova serrata*
Makino in leafless phase.
Height: 30 in.

Needle juniper/*Juniperus rigida* Sieb. et Zucc. Height: 22 in.

Satsuki azalea ''Kogetsu''/*Rhododendron indicum* Sweet in bloom.
Raft style bonsai. Height: 11 in.

Fukien tea/*Ehretia microphylla* Lamk. Dimensions: 10 in. (H) × 37 in. (W). (A bonsai chosen as a model for the R.O.C. stamp on page 42.)

Black pine/*Pinus thunbergii* Parl. Height: 36 in.

Black pine (rear view of the same bonsai on page 44).

Sargent juniper/
Juniperus chinensis L.
var. Sargenti Henry.
Height: 32 in.
(Presented as a gift from
R.O.C. President Lee
Teng-hui to the prime
minister of Singapore.)

Banyan/*Ficus microcarpa* L.f.
Height: 24 in.
(Presented as a gift to the
prime minister of Singapore.)

Sand pear/*Pyrus serotina* Rehd.
Height: 21 in.

Chinese hackberry/*Celtis sinensis* Pers. in forest-style group planting. Height: 28 in.

Common pomegranate/
Punica granatum L.
Height: 20 in.

Common pomegranate
(same bonsai as above in leafless phase).

Banyan/*Ficus microcarpa* L.f. Dimensions: 16 in. (H) × 44 in. (W).

Sargent juniper/
Juniperus chinensis L.
var. Sargenti Henry.
Height: 24 in.

Japanese flowering quince/
Chaenomeles maulei Lavall.
Length: 22 in.

Japanese gray-bark elm (zelkova)/
Zelkova serrata Makino. Height: 22 in.

Japanese gray-bark elm
(same bonsai as above in
leafless phase).

Taiwan trident maple/*Acer buergerianum* Miq.
var. formosanum (Hay.) Sasak. Height: 34 in.

Japanese premna/*Premna microphylla* Turcz. Dimensions: 11 in. (H) × 33 in. (W).

Japanese premna (same bonsai as above in leafless phase).

Satsuki azalea ''Elkan''/
Rhododendron indicum Sweet
in bloom.
Height: 15 in.

Flowering quince/
Chaenomeles lagenaria
Koidz.
Height: 14 in.

Fukien tea/*Ehretia microphylla* Lamk. Dimensions: 5 in. (H) × 14 in. (W).

Trident maple/*Acer buergerianum* Miq. Height: 24 in.

Traditional Chinese hanging landscape. Dimensions: 44 in. (W) × 21 in. (H).

Needle juniper/
Juniperus rigida Sieb. et Zucc.
Dimensions: 16 in. (H) × 21 in. (W).

Taiwan fire-thorn/
Pyracantha angustifolia Schneid.
Height: 24 in.

Philippine ebony persimmon/
Maba buxifolia (Rottb.) Pers.
Height: 34 in.

Black pine/*Pinus thunbergii* Parl. Height: 30 in.

Trident maple/*Acer buergerianum* Miq. in root-over-rock style. Height: 29 in.

Trident maple/*Acer buergerianum* Miq.
in root-over-rock arrangement.
Height: 20 in.

Formosan buckthorn/*Callicarpa formosana* Rolfe in Journ. Height: 29 in.

Black pine/*Pinus thunbergii* Parl. Length: 37 in.
(A bonsai chosen as a model for the R.O.C. stamp below.)

Sargent juniper/
Juniperus chinensis L.
var. Sargenti Henry.
Height: 37 in.

Sargent juniper/
Juniperus chinensis L.
var. Sargenti Henry.
Height: 30 in.

Japanese gray-bark elm (zelkova)/
Zelkova serrata Makino in forest-style group planting. Height: 12 in.

Japanese maple ''Deshōjō''/
Acer palmatum Thunb.
Height: 24 in.

Japanese maple
(same bonsai as above in
leafless phase).

Japanese gray-bark elm (zelkova)/*Zelkova serrata* Makino. Height: 36 in.

Japanese premna/*Premna microphylla* Turcz. Dimensions: 48 in. (H) × 33 in. (W).

Taiwan sageretia/*Sageretia thea* (Osbeck) M.C. Johnst. Height: 34 in.

Chinese elm/*Ulmus parvifolia* Jacq. Height: 18 in.

Fukien tea/*Ehretia microphylla* Lamk. Height: 14 in.

Formosan hackberry/
Celtis formosana
Hayata.
Height: 34 in.
(On display at the U.S.
Pacific Bonsai Museum.)

Needle juniper/
Juniperus rigida
Sieb. et Zucc.
Height: 32 in.

Oldham elaeagnus/*Elaeagnus oldhamii* Maxim. Height: 34 in.

Japanese gray-bark elm (zelkova)/
Zelkova serrata Makino.
Height: 18 in.

Japanese gray-bark elm
(same bonsai as above in leafless phase).

Horsetail beefwood/*Casuarina equisetifolia* Forst. Height: 35 in.

Needle juniper/
Juniperus rigida
Sieb. et Zucc.
Height: 15 in.

Horsetail beefwood/
Casuarina equisetifolia Forst.
Height: 30 in.

Needle juniper/*Juniperus rigida* Sieb. et Zucc. Height: 24 in.

Common jasmin orange/*Murraya paniculata* Jack. Height: 34 in.

Fukien tea/*Ehretia microphylla* Lamk. Height: 18 in.

Sargent juniper/
Juniperus chinensis L.
var. Sargenti Henry.
Height: 22 in.

Chinese elm/*Ulmus parvifolia* Jacq. in forest-style group planting. Height: 20 in.

Oriental arborvita/*Thuja orientalis* Linn. Height: 36 in.

Super miniature bonsai shelf display.

Display of two miniature bonsai (herb and black pine).

Display of three miniature bonsai (banyan, rock in shape of distant mountains, and trident maple).

Miniature bonsai shelf display featuring (from left to right, top to bottom) Fukien tea, herb plant, banyan, cape gardenia, Chinese elm, zelkova, and cape gardenia.

Chinese elm/*Ulmus parvifolia* Jacq. Miniature bonsai. Height: 6 in.

Display of two miniature bonsai
(black pine and herbs).

Miniature bonsai shelf display featuring (from left to right, top to bottom) cape gardenia,
figurine, trident maple, Japanese premna, herb, and Japanese flowering quince.

Trident maple/*Acer buergerianum* Miq. Miniature bonsai. Height: 8 in.

Black pine/*Pinus thunbergii* Parl. Miniature bonsai. Dimensions: 5 in. (H) × 12 in. (W).

Display of three miniature bonsai (left to right): herb, Japanese flowering quince and cape gardenia.

BONSAI, POTTED LANDSCAPES, AND LIFE

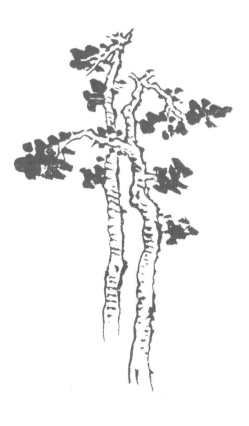

Indoor display of Japanese premna.

Bonsai, Potted Landscapes, and Life

Inquires into bonsai, potted landscapes, and potted plants

Bonsai represents the marriage of the Chinese delight for life with the art of gardening. It is the process of discovering and expressing the essence of natural trees and stones by tailoring and arranging them according to correct proportions, different growing conditions, and individual characteristics— while retaining their original nature— then reducing their volume to fit into a pot. Bonsai are man-made landscapes, the miniaturization of trees and stones in their natural state.

The word "pen-tsai," which later became "bonsai," was first used in China during the Chin Dynasty (A.D. 265 – 420); at that time, there was only "tree pen-ching,"a term that referred to potted landscapes using only trees. It was not until the Sung Dynasty (A.D. 960 – 1280) that the art of "landscape pen-ching," using decorative rocks and pavilions, was developed. This form later became known as "pen-wan." Later, in the Yuan Dynasty (A.D. 1280 – 1368), the size of landscape pen-ching was reduced; and it then became known as "little child scenes," which meant "miniature bonsai scenery." During the Ch'ing Dynasty (A.D. 1644 – 1911), miniature landscapes and trees became popular and were referred to by the name "pen-ching."

During the T'ang Dynasty (A.D. 618 – 907), the art spread to Japan. It became popular among Japanese civilians after the second World War. The Japanese transliterated the Chinese word "pen-tsai" into "bonsai." This is the name by which the form became known all over the world.

China is a vast land that is rich in resources— mountains, seas, rivers, and lakes scattered all over the country. There is an abundant supply of all kinds of rocks and trees. But in Japan, where there are fewer varieties of rocks, "landscape pen-ching" is far less advanced and popular than "tree pen-ching," which the Japanese call "bonsai."

Corner decorated with Sargent juniper.

Bonsai and stones decorating a living room.

Indoor display of Japanese flowering quince.

Indoor display of Fukien tea, Japanese flowering quince, and herb.

Bonsai incorporates the natural beauty and individuality of trees with the keenly developed aesthetic judgment and superior cultivation techniques of the expert to create a beautiful work of art that is more natural than nature itself. Merely planting trees in pots and allowing them to grow wantonly, without the beautifying influence of human creativity, yield only potted plants, not works of art.

The art of bonsai in life

Man comes from nature and to nature he returns. Therefore, man's attitude toward nature should not be to fight or conquer but to cooperate and treasure. Oriental philosophy, especially in China, was derived from the sensibility and understanding gained through human contact with nature. Among all of nature's products, trees and stones are undoubtedly the two most closely interrelated with man's living environment. If we carefully arrange lovely trees and stones in a pot, although we may not be in the midst of mountains and forests, we can nevertheless enjoy the immeasurable pleasure and wonder of nature.

Three-dimensional paintings, wordless poetry, living sculpture, living antiques

Bonsai is a unique art and has characteristics different from other arts. Bonsai may be likened to a three-dimensional painting, full of varying brushstrokes and colors. It is different from ordinary painting, however, which can only be appreciated in a single dimension. Bonsai may be enjoyed from many different angles and positions. Bonsai is also like wordless poetry. Though the bonsai tree retains its own specific characteristics, it nevertheless serves as a stimulus for the mind of the viewer to bring its own imaginings into play, and the image of the bonsai therefore lingers on in the mind. Because a bonsai has its own life force and ever-changing variety, it may be thought of as living sculpture. It may also live in the pot for decades, making it a kind of living antique.

Indoor display of Sargent juniper and black pine.

Creating a rock planting.

Wiring trunks in a group planting.

Designing a rock planting.

The role of bonsai in modern life:
Satisfying the desire for creation and beautification of the environment

Beginning with material collection, through nurturing and training the trees until they are successfully formed into shapely bonsai and displayed for appreciation and enjoyment, the process of bonsai creation involves great effort. But the sense of satisfaction and joy derived from this process is long-lasting. After finishing an artwork, the creative process of the artist ends. However, the creation of a bonsai is ongoing and lasts throughout the tree's natural life.

Displaying strong, aged-looking trees such as pines and junipers, red-leafed varieties such as trident maples and mountain maples, beautiful flowering and fruit trees, and interesting wild grasses near the door, in the living room, or in the study affords many opportunities for pleasure. A person living in a house filled with the "delights of the woods" seems to be in the midst of nature. In addition, plants help to regulate the air in the house.

Bonsai cultivation as a means of relaxation

Society has been transformed from its traditional agrarian structure to a busy and competitive industrial way of life. Once simple human relationships have become complicated, and a leisurely way of life has given way to one full of tension and strain. The characteristics of modern society often make people moody and irritable, unable to get along with one another and to meditate on serious matters. Hence, modern man needs a hobby to temper his emotions, relieve tension, and provide physical and mental relaxation. Growing bonsai provides many avenues for relaxation. In the process of creation, the bonsai grower becomes totally absorbed in his work and deeply involved in the pleasure it offers. It helps him become cheerful and relaxed.

Pruning a group planting.

The bonsai grower enjoys the opportunity to give free rein to his creativity and to infuse his thoughts and feelings in the tree. In this silent but powerful communication, he may focus his attention and forget all his worries. A superior bonsai is not made in one day. It requires years of constant care and patient training. Any negligence on the part of the grower may cause it to wither and lose branches or even die. Nevertheless, the bonsai lover benefits from this task. He can develop his ability to judge tree materials and his farsightedness in choosing ideal shapes for the trees; furthermore, years of caring for the bonsai not only enable him to cultivate his prudence and patience but also give him an opportunity to exercise and improve his health.

Wiring the branches of a Sargent juniper.

Cultural legacy and associations

In ancient times, the literati, or scholars, often met to engage in literary activities. Nowadays, bonsai enthusiasts gather together to discuss and display bonsai. Bonsai lovers are usually hospitable people; and, in their leisure time, they like to gather together to appreciate and compare bonsai as well as exchange their observations and experiences in bonsai cultivation. Through appreciating each other's bonsai and discussing the art over cups of tea, bonsai lovers have the opportunity to share artistic pleasure and the warmth of friendship. Thus, the hobby of bonsai has a beneficial influence on society and is able to promote harmony and peace.

After several decades of properly caring for and living with the bonsai grown and created with his own hands, the bonsai lover has infused it with his own feelings and personality. Once he passes away and these cherished bonsai are left to his children, the children will remember their deceased parent whenever they look at the trees. The bonsai have, therefore, become a most precious spiritual and cultural legacy.

Appreciating bonsai with the family.

Increasing personal wealth

Tree materials collected from the mountains or purchased are raw materials. Years of attentive care, creation, and constant improvement increase the beauty of the bonsai, and they then become artistic products. Bonsai are living antiques. With the passing of time and ongoing refinement, the trees acquire an aged feeling and exhibit a more appealing form. Thus they gradually accumulate spiritual and economic value.

HISTORY OF BONSAI

"Eighteen Scholars" painting (Northern Sung).

History of Bonsai

History of Chinese bonsai

Chinese bonsai originated from the gardening arts of ancient times. It is historically recorded that the Yuan Garden (Yuan P'u) was completed during the reign of the mythical Emperor Huang, indicating that the beautiful art of bonsai had existed since the earliest periods. During the Hsia, Shang, and Chou Dynasties (2205 – 255 B.C.), many advancements in the art were made. Gardening was applied to the creation of royal hunting parks such as King Chieh's Precious Jade Terrace (Yao T'ai) during the Hsia Dynasty, King Chou's Deer Terrace (Lu T'ai) during the Shang Dynasty, and King Wen's Divine Terrace (Ling T'ai) and Divine Marsh (Ling Chao) during the Chou Dynasty.

According to descriptions in the *Book of Poetry* (Shih-ching), King Wen's Divine Terrace occupied an area of 70 square miles networked with waterways diverted from nearby lakes; these formed the magnificent Divine Marsh, which served as a preserve for fish and other aquatic creatures. Large numbers of unusual flowers and rare trees were planted in gardens and fields, and many species of animals raised within their confines. From atop the Divine Terrace, vast panoramic vistas could be viewed in the day, while virtually endless tracts of beautiful landscape illuminated by starlight could be enjoyed at night.

The A-Fang Palace built by Emperor Shih of the Ch'in Dynasty has been well known historically since ancient times. To display the extent of his wealth and power, Emperor Shih constructed more than 300 huge and exquisite palaces; each was provided with a multitude of gardens planted with exotic trees so the emperor could thoroughly indulge in the pleasures of gardening.

In the *Ancient Ceremonies of the Han Dynasty* (Han-chiu-yi), it is recorded that "The wealthy Yuan Kuang-han constructed a garden at the foot of Mt. Peich'i which was four miles long from east to west and five miles long from north to south, completely intersticed with flowing rivers and stone mountains more than ten feet high." From this it may be verified that the construction of artificial mountains can be traced back to the Han Dynasty (206—221 B.C.).

The Shang Lin Park of Emperor Wu , who reigned during the Western Han Dynasty, is considered a typical royal garden preserve of the period. During his reign, Emperor Wu defeated the Hsiung-nu barbarians and subjugated the states to the west of China to consolidate imperial power. When Changan was established as the capital, all palaces therein were designed in the style of the Ch'in Dynasty. The Shang Lin Park was among the most representative of the palace gardens. From north to south, it stretched across the Wei River and was more than 300 miles wide. Shang Lin Park had seventy separate palaces and respective smaller parks within. It was designed so that each park would have gardens, each a palace, and each palace a view of the resulting scenery. In all, there were six lakes and more than 3,000 varieties of rare flowers and trees classified by the regions which had sent them as tribute. The palaces, gardens, and parks were constructed in imitation of nature, which involved the dredging of ponds and building up of mountains while harmoniously integrating the mountains with forests and rivers on a enormously grand scale.

With the establishment of the Eastern Han Dynasty, the capital was moved to Loyang. The geographical environment of Loyang was very poor; thus, when the parks there were built, it was necessary to build mountains, dredge waterways, construct islands, plant trees and grasses, and breed rare animals— with artificial gardening substituting for what was deficient in the natural scenery. Therefore, in Pan Ku's "Ode to the Western Capital" are the words, "Potent herbs thrive in winter, while vigorous trees grow in groves." In Chang Heng's verse on the "Western Capital" is the description, "Trees adorn the pavilion, fragrant plants cluster together."

In 1978, frescoes featuring bonsai were discovered near Hopei, in the graves of nobles who lived during the Later Han Dynasty of the Five Dynasties period. The frescoes had pictures of a variety of red blossoms arranged in a floral bonsai, with six of these floral bonsai placed on a five-cornered table. The red flowers, flower pots, and table (plant, container, stand)— the three primary elements of bonsai — were appropriately matched, resulting in a work of unsurpassed beauty.

The appearance of ceramic bonsai pots

High-temperature color ceramics were already in production during the Six Dynasties period, and beautiful kiln-fired black ceramic flower pots were also available.

Due to discord among the nobility, incessant warfare, and the subsequent weakening of the Chinese empire during the Western Chin Dynasty, the country fell prey to foreign invasion and the old capital of Loyang was occupied. The capital was then moved to Nanking, where the Eastern Chin Dynasty was established.

The Eastern Chin capital of Nanking was situated in a spacious, fertile borderland. Intellectuals tended to gather there for theoretical Taoist discussions, yearning to transcend the concerns of worldly existence. Though living in the city, they longed for the serenity of untamed mountains and forests. Therefore, they cultivated large gardens in the capital to create tranquil refuges from the tensions of urban life. Moreover, they planted gardens in their homes and grew bonsai. During the same period, the earliest Buddhist monasteries and temples with potted groves of trees, the so-called "Buddhist forest monasteries," began to appear in China. These further attest to the great satisfaction the ancient Chinese gained through bonsai gardening.

The appearance of the term "bonsai" in Chinese documents

The term "bonsai" is used in a famous ode of the Eastern Chin Dynasty entitled "Returning Home." It was written by T'ao Yuan-ming (365—427 A.D.) upon his return to his hometown Lili after resigning an official post. He wrote the two Chinese characters "p'en" (bon) and "tsai" (sai) in the section about enjoying the beauty of wild chrysanthemums. This is the earliest known record in the world of the word "bonsai." T'ao Yuan-ming was also the founder of the South China (Hua-nan) school of bonsai. According to ancient documents, Chinese bonsai had been treasured by aristocrats and nobles from before the Eastern Chin Dynasty (317—420 A.D.), which also means that Chinese bonsai was developed 1,000 years earlier than Japanese bonsai.

Assistants rubbing the inkstone for Su Tung-p'o, a Ch'ing Dynasty illustration by Wu Yu-ju.

"Dawn of Spring in the Han Palace," a Ming Dynasty painting by Chiu Ying.

An antique hand-painted porcelain container for bonsai.

A court lady presenting a bonsai planting as depicted in a wall mural of the tomb of the T'ang Dynasty Prince Chang Huai.

The most ancient Chinese bonsai container in existence

Chinese bonsai reached a new period of artistic development during the T'ang Dynasty (618—907 A.D.). Trees and mountains (stones) were blended in a miniature arrangement set in a bowl-sized container, becoming known at that time as a kind of "potted landscape" or "potted toy." Today, these are referred to as landscape bonsai (tsai-ching). The T'ang poet Tu Fu describes them as "A container of a square foot, with three peaks merging. A glance puts one in the wilds, and clouds seem to cling to the peaks. The perfume of lush bamboo accents fragrant wine as incense burners smolder brightly. Facing south to offer a toast, a delightful aroma fills the air." During the T'ang Dynasty, bonsai became popular among the common people and were regarded as rarities among the aristocracy. Ceramics and porcelain, including Huo Chou, Shih Chou, and Yueh Chou clays, for bonsai containers were in high demand and kilns multiplied throughout the country. Especially favored by reputation were the Ching Chou kilns of the north, which produced white porcelain wares and the Yueh Chou kilns of the south, which produced green porcelain wares. The most ancient Chinese floral bonsai pots in the world still in existence were fired in these kilns, and a number of them produced during this period are in the possession of the Peking Palace Museum.

The oldest fresco showing bonsai

In 1971, a royal burial mound was excavated in Chienling, Shenhsi. It was the tomb of Prince Chang Huai, the son of T'ang Dynasty Emperor Kao Tsung and Empress Wu Tse-t'ien. The corridor leading into the mound is lined with a mural featuring ladies in waiting presenting bonsai to an official. The bonsai container is round in shape and its contents consist of artificial mountains and tall trees bearing red fruit and green leaves. The gesture of the courtier presenting the gift suggests that bonsai were very desirable and occupied honored positions in the mansions of the nobility of the time. The tomb of Prince Chang Huai was built in the second year of Shen Lung (706 A.D.), and its mural reflects the indoor courtly life in the 8th century, while confirming that there were bonsai in China more than 1,200 years ago. In another T'ang Dynasty painting by Yen Li-pen, entitled "Tribute Offered by a Vassal," stones for bonsai mountains are pictured. The stones are attractive and seem to have been specially selected for placement in shallow containers very similar to those now used in the creation of potted landscapes.

The T'ang Dynasty poet Po Chu-i (Po Le-t'ien) once described potted landscape bonsai in a poem. He wrote "Pale green and the three colors of autumn billow forth in ancient streaks. Cut from green jade slabs, mountains are shaped like the roots of the clouds. Winds blow through depressions in the cliffs and moss lines the mouths of caves. These three peaks are miniature in size, but they are descendants of Mt. Hua." In another poem entitled the "Ten Virtues," Po idealizes them even further. "Cultivated to prolong its visage, it rids the eye of weariness and calms the mind against disturbing thoughts. Planted trees commune with season. Though close, the scene seems distant; one enters the caverns without walking and views the seacoast without searching, always in company with the welcome cool night air of summer. Able to thrive for years without end, it may be enjoyed as a virtuous pastime."

"Tribute Offered by a Vassal," a T'ang Dynasty painting by Yen Li-pen.

Offerings of bonsai, a drawing from the mural of the tomb of the T'ang Dynasty Prince Chang Huai.

衛
夫
人

千古事倍鵝攤字寶花蕊武女宗師
印池漁父馬駛寫
見毫香閒寫鳥綠不是尋常學盎書

Numerous bonsai on shelves decorating a Chinese studio, from the "Precious Paintings of Ma T'ai Collection."

Miniature bonsai containers made of Yihsing clay.

The earliest written work on bonsai in China

Kuo T'uo-t'uo was an outstanding expert on and innovator in bonsai cultivation, who wrote a three-volume work entitled *The Cultivating of Trees.* In this work he discusses in detail cultivation, pruning, and propagation. A contemporary scholar named Liu Tsung-Yuan extolled Kuo's level of knowledge in *The Biography of the Botanist Kuo T'uo-t'uo.* Based on the age of *The Cultivating of Trees,* it is apparent that Chinese writings on bonsai appeared about 1,000 years earlier than Japanese books on the subject. Moreover, in bonsai literature of the Edo period (1600—1800), Japanese sources acknowledge the contributions of "Master T'uo-t'uo" (Uekiya).

During the height of the T'ang Dynasty, Japan dispatched emissaries to China to study Chinese culture and art. Upon their return to Japan they spread what they had learned, especially during the Hakuho (672) and Tempyo (729) cultural periods. According to historical sources, it was also during the T'ang Dynasty that the peony flower and plum tree were introduced to Japan. This supports the theory that the returning emissaries also transmitted the idea of bonsai scenery viewing and cultivation so popular among the Chinese literati. The art gradually became very widespread in Japan. The earliest Japanese documentary work dealing with scenic bonsai was an illustrated scroll "A Collection of Springtime Sketches" completed about seven to eight centuries ago.

The earliest bonsai drawings in China

The art of bonsai developed to a level of high perfection during the Sung Dynasty (960—1280). Sung Dynasty bonsai were divided into "tree scene" and "mountain and river landscape" styles; both are fully depicted in the book *Towering Mountains, Green Plains* (Tung-t'ien-ch'ing-lu). The bonsai plant and stone arrangements therein featured very elaborate designs and were creations rich in poetic inspiration. Among them, the Northern Sung drawing entitled "Eighteen Scholars" is the most renowned. It is a lengthy scroll drawing showing three bonsai specimens. One is a pine tree planted in a shallow rectangular tray. Its leaves and branches overhang in a rounded growth pattern with pine needles projecting like flexible iron needles, with surface roots protruding through the topsoil, and scale-like rough bark giving the impression of a century of growth. These comprised the earliest collection of bonsai illustrations in China, and they predate the earliest Japanese renditions by several centuries.

The Sung Dynasty writers Su Tung-p'o and Lu Yu adored landscape bonsai and both composed quite a number of poems about them. In two of Su's verses, the following lines are found: "The mists and rain of the three peaks are as if situated in the palm of an immortal" and "The five peaks do not worry about the myriad elevated mountains, for today the nine ranges of Mt. Hua tower in a pot." In Lu Yu's poem "Calamus," it is written: "The calamus of Mt. Yen and the stones from Mt. K'un have been collected and arranged to lessen loneliness; inch-long roots grow densely in nine nodes — a handful of lofty value. Crystal clear springs bring out the color of the greenish pot in a manner charming enough to impress the most eminent rustic; with the mountain foliage in view daily, this object sweeps the memory of cares. The layers of roots, leaves, and shoots become better the longer one looks at them, making one regret that they were not gazed at earlier. It enables me to imbibe the wind-brought-dew and nourish my spirit as I myself age effortlessly." This graphic description of bonsai art is very inspiring. In the late Northern Sung Dynasty work *Yunlin Stones* (Yun-lin-shih-p'u) is a detailed cataloging of stones and their places of origin, characteristics and methods of excavation. There are also suggestions of how to match selected rocks with species of trees. The book is regarded as an important early source on the art of bonsai scenery.

Sung Dynasty bonsai containers were mainly made of either white or green porcelain. Among the varieties are those formed out of Ju or Chiun clays from Honan, with the most famous being the glazed bonsai trays made in Chingte, Kianghsi— examples of these are now in the collection of the National Palace Museum in Taipei. Japanese potters did not fire such clays until 1802.

During the Yuan Dynasty (1280 – 1368), there was a talented monk, Yun Shang-jen, who preferred to live the life of a recluse. He travelled extensively throughout China, visiting famous mountains and rivers to collect numerous materials for making a type of scenic bonsai called "little child scenes." Metaphorically, "little child" meant "miniature bonsai scenery." These consisted of stones, trees, flowering plants, and grasses out of which were fashioned small bridges, thatched dwellings and other scaled-down objects all arranged in a single container. Although the bonsai container was only about six inches in length, its visual impact loomed larger than life, for it was a small but complete microcosm of nature offering a view better than a thousand landscape paintings. As bonsai gradually became even more reduced in size during the Yuan Dynasty, a custom developed wherein the miniatures were displayed along with medium- and large-sized creations. The most common plantings were of pine trees, bamboo, and plum trees, which were regarded as the "three friends" that continued to flourish even in winter and were therefore highly cherished among bonsai enthusiasts. There is a detailed account of these bonsai in Liu Luan's *Jade Gourd* (Yu-shih-hu).

Thus, the enjoyment of bonsai scenery and stones as an amusing pastime was shared by rulers, nobles, and even the common people during both the T'ang and Sung Dynasties. It was a time when the types and shapes of beautiful bonsai containers multiplied significantly.

The art of bonsai continued to be highly popular during the Ming and Ch'ing Dynasties (1368—1911). Many works on bonsai scenery were written during both periods such as the Ming Dynasty author T'u Hsiang's *Study of Bonsai Trays* (K'ao-p'an-yu-lu), which features a commentary chapter on "Amusement Bonsai." In the *History of Plant Cultivation* (Ch'ang-wu-chih) by the late Ming Dynasty artist Wen Chen-heng, there are two scrolls in the section on "Amusement Bonsai" that provide complete details about the design of interior gardens and the cultivating of bonsai. Wang Hsiang-chin's *Compendium of Aromatic Plants* (Ch'un-fang-p'u) has a chapter devoted to bonsai scenery. Ch'en Hao-tzu of the Ch'ing Dynasty wrote *Flower Mirror* (Hua-ching) and included a chapter on "Types of Containers and Bonsai Methods." The *Mustard Seed Garden Painting Manual* (Chieh-tzu-yuan-hua-chuan) was coauthored by Chu Sheng, Wang Chih, and Wang Kai during the Kanghsi era of the Ch'ing Dynasty. Translated and published in Japan during the 13th year of Emperor Ch'ien Lung's reign (1748), it started a new vogue in the Japanese landscape painting

Traditional Chinese garden decorated with bonsai.

"Fortune and Peace," a Ch'ing Dynasty painting by Wu Yu-ju.

A Chekiang-style bonsai.

A Szechuan "corner bend"-shaped tree.

and became a classic work on the subject. Due to its extensive treatment of painting theory and method, the work also influenced Japanese bonsai enthusiasts and gave rise to a new style called "literati bonsai." This illustrated the thorough fusion of Chinese culture and the Japanese national traits of undeterred diligence, calmness, and willingness to transcend convention.

Schools of Chinese bonsai

China is a vast country with a long history of bonsai cultivation. Due to regional differences in local customs, geographical environment and climatic conditions, there have emerged many distinct variations in bonsai styles and techniques. Other factors include divergences in individual personality, preference, thought, outlook, and approach to the art. This has given rise to various unique schools of bonsai.

With regard to tree bonsai, the main styles are divided into a southern school and a northern school. The southern school is centered in Kwangtung but includes Kwanghsi and Fukien. It is also known as the Lingnan school of bonsai. The northern school is based in the Yangtze River basin and extends to Shanghai, Suchou, Hangchou and Yangchou. It is also known as the Su school of bonsai. A third style is represented by the Ch'uan school, which is centered in Szechuan. Variances of regional climate and personal temperament in northern and southern China constitute the main points of difference demarcating the stylistic characteristics of each respective school.

The Lingnan school (southern school)

The main characteristic of the Lingnan school is the fostering of elaborate and luxurious tree growth through the emphasis of pruning based on a "cutting the trunk, growing the branches" method. This approach to bonsai cultivation results in strong green foliage, flowing branch forking, and steady stately growth. However, it requires a relatively extended period of pruning to achieve success. The best trees to use must have excellent sprouting and growth capabilities if the "cutting the trunk, growing the branches" method is to be appropriately applied. Suitable trees include banyan, Chinese elm, Japanese gray-bark elm, Fukien tea, and common jasmin orange trees.

A traditional Lingnan school bonsai has a snake-like curved trunk, a pair of main branches extending like arms, five to seven layers of horizontal leaf growth, and a flat treetop. In principle, the tree should have a carefully arranged posture. Trees created in this style are descriptively called "ancient tree" and "military general style" bonsai.

At present, Lingnan bonsai can be found in two major forms. The first is represented by K'ung T'ai-ch'u's "big tree form," which has a straight trunk, many branches, dense growth patterns, a vigorous green hue, and the lively appearance of a huge tree growing in the wilds. The second form is attributed to the Reverend Su Jen of Hai Chuang Temple. Known as the "towering form," it is characterized by clean emaciated trunks and branches, sparse but elegant foliage, and a refined stately profile that reflects transcendence of the secular world. A few decades ago, Wu I-sun of Hong Kong finally developed a naturalistic style of this form which is not bound by convention.

The Su school (northern school)

The Su school is traditionally subdivided into the eastern and western. The eastern Su school is further comprised of the Yangchou and T'ung schools, while the western Su school consists of the Changshou and Suchou schools.

(1) The Yangchou school

The trunk and heavy branches of Yangchou school bonsai are curved, and even the shorter branches are bent so that the tips twist and turn in an extremely variegated manner – not a single inch of the branches is straight. This style has been referred to as the "flower pagoda" and "one-inch, three-bends" bonsai. Its canopy-like leaf sections are typically in the shape of "thin clouds" layered in odd numbered quantities. The leaf sections are not perfectly spherical; the first three lower levels are pruned in the shape of a "platform" form; and, from the fourth level upward, in a "delicate cloud" form.

(2) The T'ung school

The T'ung school branch training method is similar to that of the Yangchou school, except that the trunk has a circular bend starting from the roots in the bonsai container. This is followed by two similar semi-circular bends in the upper trunk, which are described as "two half-bends" in the nomenclature of the school. The T'ung school is based in Anhwei. In addition to the characteristic of two half-bends, trees are planted so that they incline forward. The most commonly chosen trees are Chinese cypress and Sargent juniper. Due to its S-shaped left and right bends, the trunk resembles a winding dragon and is aptly called the "coiled dragon" form.

(3) The Changshou school

Typical Changshou school bonsai can be found in Changshou, Nanking, Wuhsi, and other nearby locations. These bonsai traditionally consist of the merging of "six platforms, three bases and one tip." Trunks are trained to attain six alternating bends, with each protruding bend referred to as a platform. The three main branches growing toward the rear are called the three bases; these accentuate the single tip at the top of the tree. Foliage on the branches is pruned to form a circular shape, and the cultivator must keep the bark unharmed and intact to achieve the ideal appearance.

(4) The Suchou school

The Suchou school extends to include the Shanghai region. In addition to featuring the "six platforms, three bases and one tip" influence of the Changshou school, bonsai of the Suchou school integrates "coarse wiring and fine pruning" to achieve an S-shaped branch growth that becomes increasingly dense following years of careful trimming. The most notable bonsai shapes of this school are the "tree branches overhanging a cliff" and "windswept branches" forms. The latter form is similar to the "slanted trunk" form, but the angle of the trunk is more extreme and an overly extended branch protrudes abruptly at the top. Pine trees are often used in this type of bonsai, and they are often placed in living rooms because they mimic a beckoning gesture that is

A tradition Szechuan-style shaped tree.

The "two half-bend" tree shape of the T'ung school.

easily observed by guests. Such creations are called "guest welcoming pines."

The Shanghai school style is renowned for delicate and exquisitely-trained bonsai planted in containers no larger than the palm of the hand. In the past few decades, the well-known experts Chou Shou-shih, Chu Tzu-an, and other proponents of the Suchou school have developed a new thematic design that emphasizes natural beauty.

The Ch'uan school

The Ch'uan school is regionally centered in Chengtu, and its bonsai are characterized by many flowing curves attained through branch training. These include what are called "corner bends," "reversing curves," "greatly bowed overhanging branches," "coiled dragons around a staff," and "wife applying make-up" forms. Other curved branch forms are the "flat," "coiled," and "semi-flat semi-coiled"; collectively, they are referred to as "earthworm curves."

There are many schools of Chinese bonsai that reflect distinctive regional characteristics. Since the artistic methods and cultivating techniques are unequalled anywhere, as well as being rooted in 5,000 years of cultural history, they are destined to make a significant contribution to the international bonsai world.

Bonsai of Taiwan

During the Ch'ing Dynasty, bonsai were enjoyed by educated gentlemen residing in the vicinity of the provincial cities of Tainan, Lukang, and Mengchia (the present day district of Wanhua in Taipei). Today, bonsai and bonsai pots more than two centuries old can be found in Tainan's Kaiyuan Temple, Lukang's Matsu Temple, and Taipei's Lungshan Temple.

The last few decades have brought Taiwan societal stability, economic development, and national prosperity. In order to enhance the environment, the government sponsored a national plant-beautification project. Starting on May 20, 1984, it presented an educational program on public television entitled "The Art of Chinese Bonsai in Taiwan." The 13-part series was telecast over a period of four months, and the author was called on to provide narration for the installments. The series was re-telecast due to an overwhelming response from viewers. The number of bonsai enthusiasts has increased to over 150,000 people throughout the nation. The number of bonsai clubs and associations has risen to more than 60; each year they support more than 100 bonsai exhibitions. Through the coordination and encouragement of provincial and municipal authorities, interest in bonsai has reached new heights, and its popularity is still increasing. In Taiwan, bonsai cultivation has gradually become a leisure activity.

Taiwan is blessed with a favorable climate characterized by moderate temperatures and humidity. Because it spans both tropical and subtropical zones, even the highest mountainous regions have temperate belts. Thus, the island offers a suitable environment for a wide variety of wild plants that require naturally fertile soil. The ideal climate also enables plants to grow rapidly, survive longer and be easier to prune into desired shapes. Compared to nations located in the frigid zone, in which it may take up to ten years to grow a completed bonsai, it takes only three to five years to accomplish the same in Taiwan. Because it does not snow in

The Lin Family Garden in Wufeng, Taichung.

The winding corridors of the Lin Pen-yuan estate in Panchiao, Taipei.

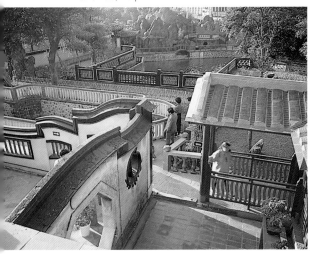

winter, local bonsai cultivators are spared the time and expense of sheltering plants once a year. Bonsai raised in Taiwan continue to grow and flourish throughout the winter months.

Banyans were once the main trees used in bonsai in Taiwan. Branches were usually kept short, while foliage growth was pruned to form flat level sections. Banyans were often trained in the shape of common objects such as gourds, animals, and Chinese characters; however, even this departure from natural forms can become somewhat monotonous. Chinese elm, Japanese grey-bark elm, common jasmin orange, Taiwan fire-thorn, Fukien tea, trident maple, mountain maple, and Chinese hackberry have in recent years been taken from the mountains and transplanted into bonsai pots. Pine and juniper trees are relative newcomers to Taiwan, but they have become another popular choice in local bonsai cultivation. As living space has become smaller, miniature bonsai have now become increasingly fashionable.

Bonsai pruning methods in Taiwan are outgrowths of the "cutting the trunk, growing the branches" method of the Lingnan school, which emphasizes natural characteristics. When grown in Taiwan's ideal climate, the foliage becomes thick and luxuriant, lending itself to countless possibilities in the innovative creation of bonsai. Thus, local variation in the art has advanced and flourished.

From the "Real People Paintings Collection by Wu Yu-ju."

Bonsai of Japan

The earliest illustrations of bonsai in Japan are found in *Natural Methods of Figure Painting* (1300), *A Collection of Springtime Sketches* (1304), and *An Outline of Bonsai* (1892). These works contain pictures of the types of bonsai existing in Japan at the time.

In Japan, the earliest essay on bonsai was Yoshida Kenko's (1330 – 1341) "Picking Natural Plants," a recorded discussion on various species of flora. The term "bonsai" is frequently found on scrolls of 19th-century landscape paintings. In Abe Kijin's (1821) *Propagating Plants and Trees,* bonsai is mentioned along with notes explaining the Japanese pronunciation "hachiue," which means potted plant.

In 1827, Shokin Taisho wrote "Renowned Plant Cultivators," which includes a fine collection of bonsai drawings. This work was followed in 1836 by Saito Ichizaemon's *Paintings of Famous Places in Edo,* which contains illustrations of bonsai displayed at temple fairs.

The Japan Bonsai Association published *Illustrations of Japanese Bonsai.* Iwas Ryoji's "A Short History of Japanese Bonsai" is included as the final chapter. It presents historical evidence of the transmittal of Chinese bonsai to Japan.

In the mid-18th century, Japanese bonsai progressed from the "rusticated" form to the "refined" form, eventually developing into the "aesthetic beauty bonsai" form. The renowned bonsai expert Kobayashi Norio in 1921 introduced yet another formal variation called "natural bonsai."

During the early 20th-century Anglo-Japanese Alliance, Japanese bonsai were often exhibited in Great Britain. The exhibitions were usually sponsored by the London Society for the Promotion of Gardening Arts. In 1910, Japanese bonsai were displayed at the Britain-Japan Fair.

Some of Japan's finest bonsai were displayed at the 1964 World Olympics held in Tokyo and Expo '70 in Osaka. These specimens were instrumental in giving impetus to the popularity of the art in modern times.

Prospective buyers examining bonsai at the flower market.

CHINESE ROCK PLANTING

The skyline and scenery of Kueilin.

Magnificent natural cavern scenery.

Chinese Rock Planting

Chinese landscapes are well-known all over the world. Chinese people are fond of nature and embrace it fully. They like to enjoy the beauty of mountains and rivers, and rock planting gives them the opportunity to do this at home. Rocks may, therefore, be combined with trees, bowers, bridges, human figures, birds, animals, and moss in shallow water containers to imitate the beauty of nature. Rocks serve as the symbol of mountains. It is important that all decorative materials, which are reflected in the water, be unified. Rock plantings allow their owners to enjoy the pleasure of nature by imagining they are outdoors.

Types of Rock Planting

Mountains have different shapes, each of which have their own characteristics.

The layout of rock plantings may be classified into single peak, double peak, group peak, island, cliff, river, etc.

The production methods of rock planting are as follows:

(1) Soil rock planting: Only soil without water in the container.

(2) Water rock planting: Only water without soil in the container.

(3) Soil-and-water rock planting.

(4) Soil-and-sand rock planting: Sand is used as the symbol of the water surface in this style. Soil in the container is the symbol of land.

Rock planting may exhibit three different perspectives:

(1) Eye-level perspective: Looking at distant mountains from the point where you stand.

(2) Upward perspective: Looking at the peak from the foot of a mountain.

(3) Deep perspective: Looking at a mountain from the front to the back.

The perspective is dependent upon variation in the height, width, and depth of the rock planting.

"Clustered peaks" style
rock planting.

"Mountain peak" style
rock planting.

"Horizontal strata" style
rock planting.

Soil-and-water rock planting.

"Angled" style rock planting.

"Valley" style rock planting.

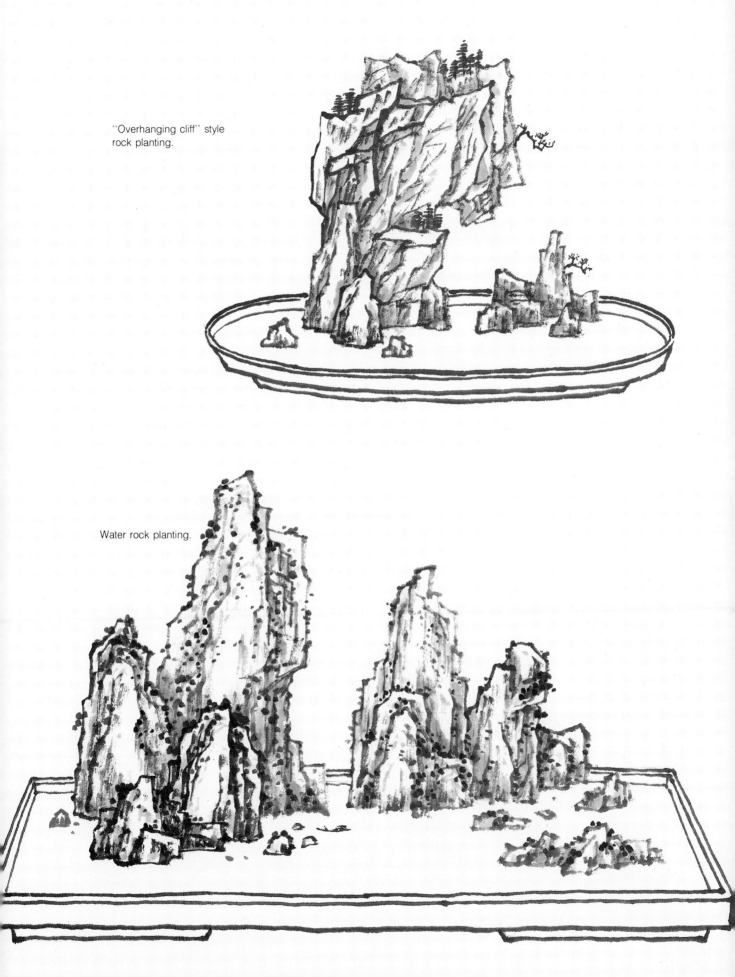

"Overhanging cliff" style rock planting.

Water rock planting.

Irregular surface often seen on mountain stones

Choose suitable rock materials

Chinese people favor mountains and rocks because they symbolize strength, stability, and immortality. They are also full of variety and aesthetic interest.

Natural rocks have different structures, shapes, and surface textures, which are enhanced by the weathering effect of wind, rain, ice, frost, and the sand in water. Rocks can be grouped into three categories, according to formative causes: fire rock, water rock, and degenerative rock. Rocks can also be classified into hard rock (e.g. stalactite, inkstone, and turtle-grain stone) and soft rock. Hard rock has a dense degree of coagulation, a fine texture and is slick, while soft rock has a loose and soft texture that is subject to wind penetration and can be damaged easily.

Rocks are named according to their surface characteristics:

(1) Stone skin and stone flesh: After penetration by water, the soft part of the stone skin may peel off, and the remainder is called stone flesh, which is slick and shiny.

(2) Beehive appearance: Rock degenerated underground due to heat, gas, and hot water will have a surface full of small holes that looks like a beehive.

(3) Rice spotted: Rocks in which spots resembling rice grains swell up on the surface.

(4) Grained: Rocks that have different patterns in the texture of the surface.

(5) Wrinkled: Rocks that have folds like waves on the surface.

(6) Striped: Rocks that have dents or convex streaks like snake-shaped lines on the surface.

(7) Permeating veins: Rocks that have graphite veins running through them to form vivid patterns.

In the Ming Dynasty, Kung Hsien (a famous stone collector) wrote descriptions of stones. He said that round stones should have angles and square stones should have layers. In addition to three essential components— quality, shape, and color— there are five characteristics of fine rocks. They are as follows:

(1) There should be drainage passages on the rock surface.

(2) There should be holes, dented or convex, on the rock surface.

(3) The rock should be thin and straight to show strength and magnificence.

(4) The texture of the rock surface should be full of variety.

(5) Various patterns of rock might be engaging even though they are technically ugly.

The selection of rock is based on two terms: fantastic and beautiful. The former refers to forms that are ingenious and elegant, and the latter to those that are refined and pretty.

The rock materials in rock planting should have hard textures, beautiful patterns, and graceful shapes that are appropriate for display in containers. Uncut mountain rock is the best choice. Rock materials with loose and soft textures that are easy to cut and polish may also be used. They absorb water easily for growing moss.

Stones rounded by rushing streams are most common.

Strip-eroded irregularities.

Wrinkled hemp cloth irregularities.

Cumulous cloud irregularities.

Axed irregularities.

Loosened knot irregularities.

Scattered firewood and hemp
irregularities.

"Valley" style rock planting.

"Clustered peak" style rock planting.

"Mountain peak" style rock planting.

"Lakes and marshes" style rock planting.

Mountains should be accompanied by water

Water and mountains represent softness and hardness, respectively. Together, they thoroughly represent the beauty of nature. Water is a symbol of the source of life and the lifeblood of the mountains. Without water, mountains seem lifeless. In rock plantings, water, used to suggest rivers and lakes, makes the design more attractive and complete.

Mountains, water, containers, and stands

Water containers are very important in rock planting. They can be pottery pots, china pots, brass pots, or others.

The stand is the table where the rock planting containers are displayed. Stands should be made of red sandalwood, black sandalwood, or Chinese quince wood to best set off the rock planting. The size of the container and the table should be in proportion. The best effect may be achieved if the container is about two-thirds the size of the table.

The area of the rock in the layout should be one-third the size of the container. Big and high rocks fit well in deep containers, small or short rocks in shallow ones. Sand added to the container should not be too white or it will look unnatural.

The position of the rock in a container is critical. If the shape of the rock leans left, the rock should be placed in the right of the container. The design of the rock stretch upward and lean slightly to the front. If the rock leans backward, the layout will be awkward and unstable, because of the same principle that dictates cultivation of a bonsai tree.

If the layout of the rock planting is designed to develop perspective, mountains with single peaks, double peaks, adjacent peaks, or overlapping peaks can be imitated. The key to perspective design is an appreciation of the spirit and vigor of the mountains. It is important to design the layout with the height of the mountains in correct proportions.

Single peaks: The rock should be positioned off-center, dividing the container in two parts with proportions of 4:6 or 3:7. To show strength, the rock must have a dynamic and well-defined edge contour. Water, soil, and sand can be arranged around the rock.

Double peaks: The ratio of the main peak to the sub-peak should be about 2:8 or 3:7. The two should overlap slightly.

Adjacent peaks: It is important to avoid arrangements in which front peaks are higher than rear peaks because the rocks in front will obscure those in the rear. The slope of the mountains should be gradual in this style to best display the spatial relationship between the peaks.

Overlapping peaks: Because mountains overlap from low to high, from near to far, the slopes of the rocks in this arrangement should rise and fall naturally, and the tips of the mountains should incline forward slightly.

If the rock planting is designed to express a view at close range, the patterns and shapes of the rocks, the grass or trees, and the display of water are critical. For example, in a layout where an old man is fishing on a platform adjacent to a mountain and water plants are in the distance with two or three cranes on them, the following should be observed:

(1) The main peak should be stronger and more expressive than the sub-peak.

(2) The peaks of the mountains should incline forward slightly.

(3) The mountain peaks must not fall backward, or the composition will lose its strength.

(4) The mountain peaks should be proportionate, or the entire arrangement will appear disorderly.

(5) Do not add too many decorations to the rock planting, or it will become disorderly and dull.

(6) The distance between a hillside and the foot of a mountain cannot be too great, or the arrangement will be disorderly.

(7) Choose long and shallow containers to give the impression of a wide and deep view.

No matter how many rocks are placed in a rock planting, their positions and the distance between them should be dynamic and natural. The overall arrangement must be harmonious.

Stages in designing a rock planting:
(1) Positioning the main peak.
(2) Arranging the supplementary peaks.
(3) Completing the layout.

"Ocean and island" style rock planting.

"Valley" style rock planting.

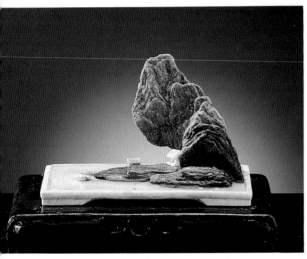

"Overhanging cliff" style rock planting.

"Double peak" style rock planting.

An exquisitely delicate rock planting (same rock planting on the left).

An exquisitely delicate rock planting (same rock planting on the left).

Trees, decorations, and moss

Trees

Trees may be compared to the clothes of the mountains. In the western world, trees are regarded as useful and enjoyable things. Chinese people, however, have more complex attitudes toward trees, which they believe reflect their thoughts and feelings.

In rock plantings, the positions in which trees are planted are based on the rules of perspective. For example, plant a small pine on a cliff-like mountain to show the tree's spirit, which is lonely but proud, or plant a willow beside the mountain and the water to create the impression of swinging leaves. To show the massiveness of a rock, put a small, low stone beside a high, narrow one to achieve contrast. It is better to choose small, trained trees to plant on rocks. The smaller the tree, the larger the rock will appear. Plant trees with dense leaves (such as Hinoki cypress or Sargent juniper) around a rock to create the illusion of a winding path and a valley. To suggest wilderness, plant several individual elm trees in the pot, leaving wide spaces between them. For a seashore scene, plant some small trees leaning to one side to create the illusion that winds are blowing into the shore and the trees are swinging in them.

It is also important to preserve different levels among trees and rocks. Some space should be reserved for decorations. For instance, trees around a house should be planted wide apart to emphasize the size of the yard. Plant some tall trees beside a pavilion; the trees leaning toward the pavilion become a sunshade.

A rock planting of miniaturized natural scenes.

"Solitary island" style rock planting.

Decorations

Decorations include human figures, bridges, boats, pavilions, birds, and animals, which must be placed in appropriate positions. Apply the rules of near-high-big and far-low-small to make the scene appear larger. For example, put boats of different sizes near and far in a water container to create the illusion of distance. Do not place too many trees and decorations in the layout, or the major subject of the layout will not stand out. In a rock planting, rocks, trees, and decorations should be in proportion to one another to create perspective. Viewers should be allowed space to appreciate the creation through their own various visual responses.

Moss

Moss is a very important supporting material in rock planting. Chang Chao, a poet in the Ch'ing Dynasty, wrote that rocks should not exist without moss. Moss can be ground with water into paste and brushed on a wet rock, which must be put in a shady and humid place. Spray water on the rock regularly. Green moss will start to grow on the rock in a short time. It is necessary to trim the moss on the rock often. Moss should be most dense in a dent or a dark place on the rock. Moss in bright positions or facing sunshine should not grow too densely. Remember not to grow too much moss in order to keep the texture of the rock visible.

Sculpted wood scene.

Creation of landscapes using rocks

It is important to cultivate a sense of aesthetics in rock planting. Rock planting affords the opportunity to recreate natural scenery in a small pot to present the spirit and beauty of the mountains and water. The mystery of rock planting is in its ability to miniaturize nature. Anyone who wants to be successful in the creation of rock plantings should observe nature often, photograph natural landscapes, and study masterpieces of rock planting. Try to understand and imitate real scenery carefully and thoroughly. Once the shapes of various mountains are imprinted on the mind, it will be possible to create fine works without undue effort.

Make sure the views to be presented correspond to the natural shapes of rock materials. Then, begin to design the layout and create the desired scene.

Creating a rock planting:
(1) Preparing the proper materials.
(2) Marking positions for mountain stones.
(3) Positioning mountain stones.
(4) Placing the trees.

Choose rocks with similar qualities, colors, and textures. Clean the surface of each rock to reveal its texture, and cut the bottom evenly. It is also possible to cut the rock into two parts (one-third and two-thirds of its area). The larger part may be used as the main peak and the smaller the sub-peak.

Dark-colored fine rocks best show the graceful characteristics of rock plantings. Stones with light or bright colors that irritate the eye or those with unclear colors should not be used. Nowadays, many people apply oil or wax to the surface of rocks to enhance brightness and color, but this makes the arrangement less natural. The rocks become artificial and dull. This is a mistake that should, therefore, be avoided.

The layout of the creation should follow the shapes of the rocks. High and straight rocks can be used to form a valley. Imagine the following landscapes: mountains of various heights facing each other are bisected by a path. A woodcutter is coming back from the mountains and a cowboy is playing a flute under a tree. A flock of sheep is eating grass. A high rock and a platform can evoke the impression of someone fishing beside a lake. These scenes, full of the joy of nature, can be suggested by rock plantings.

The main peak is usually positioned at a point one-third of the way from the left or the right of the container. If the shape of the rock leans left, position the rock on the right; if it leans right, position it on the left. Sub-peaks and supporting peaks should be positioned in the form of an unequal triangle to prevent dullness. The tips of these peaks should be positioned in such a way that they present an impressive and harmonious picture.

The general rule for the arrangement of rocks is as follows: High peaks should be impressive and stand out. Distant views should overlap and possess less definite outlines. Near views can be created through the use of fine sand, which produces a feeling of space and infinity. The texture of rocks in near views should be delicate; rocks in the distance should appear obscure and mysterious.

In sum, materials used in rock planting should be positioned in proper proportions and rise above the water surface. The objective is to display various heights and the distance and slopes of mountains. The size of trees and the flow of water should also be taken into consideration.

Captions

Captions in rock planting often have surprising power to illuminate the subject of a work. A caption should be simple and poetic. There are two ways to write captions:

(1) Entity caption: The topic and scenery of a work may be easily discerned from its caption.

(2) Sense caption: This kind of caption allows people to use their own imaginations to interpret the scenery of a work. The caption cannot, however, be arbitrary but should match the scene.

The maintenance of rock plantings

Finished works should be put in a shady and humid place. A place near a sunny part of the house is best because plants will remain green with little trouble. It is important to trim and train the plants on the rock often. Make sure that they stay in proportion to the rock to maintain a graceful appearance. If necessary, spray with water and apply fertilizers regularly to encourage the growth of the plants. In order to maintain brightness and beauty, wash away dust that may obscure the pleasing texture of the rock material.

Completed rock planting creation.

(5) Miniature deer decoration.
(6) Crane flock decoration.
(7) Figurine decoration.
(8) Village dwelling decoration.

THE CLASSIFICATIONS
OF BONSAI

The unique beauty of a tree in nature and the beauty of a bonsai planting are mutually related.

Bonsai originated from the art of gardening.

The Classifications of Bonsai

The art of bonsai cultivation is derived from the Chinese traditional art of garden planning, which can be classified into two main categories:

Landscape bonsai: A realistic way of presenting the beauty of rocky landscapes by integrating rocks, the chief material, with trees, figurines, pavilions, bridges, boats, animals, etc., as decorative material.

Tree bonsai: Trees, the chief materials, are integrated with rocks, grass, moss, and ornaments that are used as decorative material to imitate real trees. Trees are trained and shaped to display the essence and various characteristics of different species.

There are many kinds of bonsai. Bonsai are generally classified by the shape, number, height, and species of trees as well as by quality.

Classification of trees in bonsai appreciation

Classification chart of common bonsai varieties

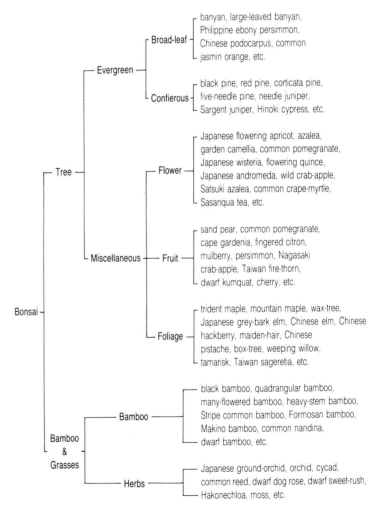

Bonsai
- Tree
  - Evergreen
    - Broad-leaf — banyan, large-leaved banyan, Philippine ebony persimmon, Chinese podocarpus, common jasmin orange, etc.
    - Confierous — black pine, red pine, corticata pine, five-needle pine, needle juniper, Sargent juniper, Hinoki cypress, etc.
  - Miscellaneous
    - Flower — Japanese flowering apricot, azalea, garden camellia, common pomegranate, Japanese wisteria, flowering quince, Japanese andromeda, wild crab-apple, Satsuki azalea, common crape-myrtle, Sasanqua tea, etc.
    - Fruit — sand pear, common pomegranate, cape gardenia, fingered citron, mulberry, persimmon, Nagasaki crab-apple, Taiwan fire-thorn, dwarf kumquat, cherry, etc.
    - Foliage — trident maple, mountain maple, wax-tree, Japanese grey-bark elm, Chinese elm, Chinese hackberry, maiden-hair, Chinese pistache, box-tree, weeping willow, tamarisk, Taiwan sageretia, etc.
- Bamboo & Grasses
  - Bamboo — black bamboo, quadrangular bamboo, many-flowered bamboo, heavy-stem bamboo, Stripe common bamboo, Formosan bamboo, Makino bamboo, common nandina, dwarf bamboo, etc.
  - Herbs — Japanese ground-orchid, orchid, cycad, common reed, dwarf dog rose, dwarf sweet-rush, Hakonechloa, moss, etc.

Black pine.

Common jasmin orange.

Japanese flowering quince.

Horsetail beefwood.

Trident maple.

Japanese wisteria.

Needle juniper.

Dwarf kumquat.

Japanese maple ''Deshōjō.''

Oriental arborvita.

Sargent juniper.

Fukien tea.

Chinese podocarpus.

Satsuki azalea.

Azalea.

Maiden-hair.

Classification by number of trees

Generally speaking, there are two categories of bonsai based on the number of trees in the design. These are called single-trunk and multiple-trunk.

The single-trunk bonsai style includes upright, slanting, and coiled designs.

The multiple-trunk bonsai style includes twin-trunk, three-tree, five-tree, seven-tree, group planting, clump, and raft designs.

Classification by height of trees

Because the environments in which bonsai are grown differ, there are varying opinions about which bonsai size is most desirable. The following size classifications are commonly acknowledged:

Extra large bonsai: 36 in. — 60 in. In spacious garden courtyards or large-scale exhibitions, extra large bonsai look strong and imposing. They were in vogue once; but, as living space has become smaller, they have gradually become less popular.

Large bonsai: 30 in. — 36 in. A large bonsai takes at least two people to move. At present, the large bonsai is the most favored size. Large bonsai best display the aesthetic character, dignity, and grace of this art form and are most suitable for bonsai lovers living in spacious houses.

Various types of herbal bonsai.

Extra large bonsai (Satsuki azalea).

Large bonsai (Common jasmin orange).

Taiwan fire-thorn.

Medium bonsai (Box-tree).

Miniature bonsai (Cape gardenia).

Super miniature bonsai (Dwarf dog rose).

Super miniature bonsai maintained in a greenhouse.

Medium bonsai: 12 in. — 30 in. Currently, this is the most popular type of bonsai. A bonsai of this size can be easily carried in two hands, and its care and maintenance are also manageable. Furthermore, it can be positioned near the door, in the living room, on a small table, or in the hallway. Medium bonsai are the most popular type in the international market and are sold at high prices. They also have the highest appreciated value and are the best medium for exhibiting the horticultural art of bonsai experts.

Small bonsai: Below 12 in. A small bonsai is very convenient in terms of control and enjoyment; it can be carried in one hand and placed on a small table, on a desk, or in a small room. For bonsai enthusiasts who live in cities and have limited living space, small bonsai are the most suitable size. Today, as living space shrinks, small bonsai are beginning to arouse the attention of bonsai lovers at home and abroad. Since small bonsai, especially the miniature bonsai between 6 in. and 8 in. can be trained and styled without much trouble, they are destined to become as popular as the medium bonsai in the near future.

Super miniature bonsai: About 4 in. Super miniature bonsai are so small that several of them can be carried in one hand. They are exquisitely delicate. Their small size prevents them from fully presenting the characteristics of bonsai; furthermore, they are not easy to manage. Hence, there is no way to promote them, and they have few admirers. They are, however, a suitable size for bonsai lovers living in apartments.

Classification by quality

Bonsai can be grouped into two categories based on quality: superior bonsai and common bonsai.

Superior bonsai: The following should be taken into consideration when the quality of a superior bonsai is judged. There should be no serious defects in the root-base, trunk-base, trunk, branches, foliage, inflorescence, fruit, the overall shape of the tree, and the proportion of the design. In addition, the bonsai should evoke in the viewer feelings of unity, serenity, and stability. There should also be variety in the arrangement of space. A superior bonsai should be a perfect creation, bearing no trace of artificiality and yet possessing more charm than nature itself. Finally, the tree should be old and adaptable to more than two climatic zones.

Common bonsai: A common bonsai is a tree that has large cuts in the front, unsightly surface roots, disagreeable branch lines, no harmony in the thickness of the branches and trunk, abnormal height, bad design proportion, traces of artificiality, and poor adaptability to climatic zones or be a tree material with a short life span (such as bamboo or grass).

The author has often heard people remark that there is no absolute standard for judging the quality of bonsai because personal taste and opinion vary. As a matter of fact, one has only to display two bonsai of differing quality side by side to determine which is superior and which inferior. Bonsai enthusiasts should go to the mountains often to observe trees in their natural state and extract from them the reasons for their natural beauty— then apply this knowledge to overcome weaknesses in bonsai design. A bonsai surpassing nature in beauty is the desired result. There is, therefore, no such thing as varying standards of bonsai quality; only technique may vary.

Super miniature fruit tree bonsai (Nagasaki crab-apple).

Medium fruit tree bonsai (Dwarf kumquat).

Small flowering bonsai (Japanese flowering quince).

BASIC STYLES OF BONSAI

Natural scene of a nearly perfect vertical trunk.

Expansive horizontal branches of a tree in a natural setting.

Basic Styles of Bonsai

The basic styles of bonsai can be roughly classified into the following: upright, slanting, coiled, twisted trunk, cascade, literati, weeping, exposed-root, clump, twin-trunk, straight-line or raft, wind-swept, broom, group planting, tray-landscape, clinging-to-a-rock and root-over-rock styles.

Upright style

With this style, the root-base radiates vigorously outward. A tree with an erect trunk is called a formal upright style, whereas a tree with a slightly curved trunk is called an informal upright style. The trunk of an upright style should be thick at the base and taper toward the top; furthermore, it should be round and without wounds. With the upright style, there must be one thick and strong main branch on the lower portion of the trunk. The ideal starting position of the first branch is approximately 1/3 of the way up the trunk. The rest of the branches should alternate in an orderly spiral pattern. Toward the top the branches should be closer together and vary according to the width of the root-base. No branch should be allowed to grow below the 1/3 point on the front of the trunk in order for the tree to exhibit massiveness. The whole tree should form an asymmetrical triangle. On the wider side of the root-base, branches should be long, and short on the narrower side. Suitable tree species are common cryptomeria, Hinoki cypress, needle juniper, common jasmin orange, and pine. The upright style best exhibits strength, majesty, and stability. This style looks best in oval and rectangular pots.

Slanting style

A tree whose apex leans either to the left or the right is called a slanting style. If, however, the trunk slants too much, it will convey a sense of instability. Therefore, the angle of the trunk should not exceed 30 degrees. Also, the length of the branches may be managed to help maintain the tree's balance and lend variety to the overall shape. On the side of the slant, there should be comparatively longer, dragging branches; on the opposite side, the branches should be denser. Compression on the side of the lean encourages the roots on this side to take the form of a buttress, and they are called compressive roots. On the opposite side, where a pulling or tensile force is at work, the roots are called tensile roots. The overall shape of the tree should be in a slight curve. If the trunk slants toward the right, branches on that side should generally be heavier; if the trunk bends toward the left, the center of gravity should be slightly to the left. With the trunk slanting to one side and the foliage and branches in a pleasing arrangement, the slanting style can be very charming and picturesque. Suitable tree species are black pine, five-needle pine, Chinese elm, and Chinese hackberry. Shallow oval or rectangular pots are ideal for this style.

Coiled style

A coiled style bonsai is made of a tree with a completely twisted trunk. Its apex will bend slightly to the front. In this style, the roots spread out in every direction. If the base of the trunk slants to one side, the roots on that side must be comparatively longer and stronger. In this style the trunk coils in a graceful shape, the foliage is lush, and the tree tapers toward the top. Branches should not, however, be too long; the ideal length is eight to ten times the diameter of the trunk so that trunk and branches are agreeably balanced. The coiled style possesses a refined, lively, and aged appearance— the most natural shape found among trees grown in mountains and on plains. Any species of tree may be used to create the coiled style. Oval or rectangular pots are preferable.

The gnarled trunk and branches of a Sargent juniper.

Twisted-trunk style

Trees that grow on mountains or island rocks and are exposed to constant strong winds and snow, that endure earthquakes and the pressure of the land for many years, have gnarled and twisted trunks. The turns and loops of the twisted-trunk style create a very interesting pattern. Some parts of the trunk and branches may have withered up, forming silvery grey bark or "shari" (meaning "Buddha ashes" or "holy relics"). Dry branches have an antique appearance. Some of the wounds heal over and form knots, while others swell or hollow in. If used carefully, these characteristics can be used to create a masterpiece of bonsai. Oval or rectangular pots are suitable for this style. The Sargent juniper and black pine are the most commonly used species.

An overgrowth of vegetation and moss gives this tree an ancient air.

Cascade style

Trees that grow on precipitous mountains, broken ridges, on steep cliffs, or along the coast are exposed to the destructive forces of earth movements and severe snowstorms. In such harsh and perilous environments, trees cling precariously to ledges of rock above precipices. In order to gain more sunlight and space, they struggle to stretch out their branches; thus they develop very pleasing and varied shapes. In addition, because the weight of the whole tree tends downward, the trunk bends over and the branches hang over the edge of the cliff. Bonsai in this style planted in the courtyard can make the owner think of "above are broken ridges; below is running water" — a very poetic and picturesque image. If the branches do not reach the level of the bottom of the pot, the tree is called a semi-cascade. If the branches reach below the level of the bottom of the pot, the tree is called a full cascade. Any tree species may be used to create a cascade style. The pot should be deep or semi-deep.

Natural scenery of willows waving in the wind.

Literati style

This style was the favorite of the literati in ancient China. Trees in this style grow in valleys between precipices or beside mountain streams. The trunk is slender, tall, and graceful. As a result of low sunlight, the trunk has no branches on its lower part. Branches are sparse and short with many open spaces between them, giving the tree the appearance of fragility, elegance, and unworldly grace. The literati is the easiest style to create, but it is, at the same time, difficult to accomplish well. The artist must possess three qualities to make the choices necessary to create a successful literati style: keen aesthetic judgment, accumulated wisdom, and superb techniques. Favorable tree species are trees of the pine and juniper families, maple, Japanese flowering apricot (plum), Fukien tea, and Oldham elaeagnus. Shallow round or irregular pots of austere color should be chosen for this style to display a peaceful and relaxed feeling.

Weeping style

"A thousand twigs sway in the breeze." In this style, the trunk should be tall and display some variety, either informal upright or slanting. The branches should bend downward and spread out from a high position in one single direction or in all directions. (Generally, trees that spread downward to two or three times the depth of the pot are called full-weeping styles; trees that reach down to the bottom of the pot are called semi-weeping styles.) A very charming and poetic tree shape with soft weeping branches may be created in this way. Suitable species are weeping willow and Oldham elaeagnus. This style looks best in round or irregular pots.

Exposed-root style

Trees growing in the crevices of rocks develop exposed roots when the wind and rain have weathered the surface rocks near their root bases; trees along the seashore or river also form exposed roots once the surface sand is washed away. The twisted roots that are exposed to the air and sunshine become strong enough to support the whole weight of the tree without any substantial foundation. Such natural magic at work on trees often inspires wonder. Roots of bonsai can be developed artificially by inserting the root into a bamboo tube and filling the tube with sand or soil. When the roots expand into the soil or the bottom of the pot and become stronger, the bamboo tube can be cut away. Any species of tree can be used for this style. Pots should be round, oval, or rectangular.

A natural tree scene of coarse, slanted roots.

Clump style

In this style, at least three trunks grow out from the roots of the tree and resemble a woodland. The point where the trunks separate from each other should be above the root-base but not too high up. The thickness, height, and shape of trunks should be different. The arrangement of the trunks and branches should have the effect of harmony and unity. For some species, cutting the trunk-base helps it sprout and create new trunks. Species most commonly used are pine, Chinese elm, Chinese hackberry, flowering quince, mountain maple, and Fukien tea. Oval or square pots are suitable for this style.

Twin-trunk style

In this style, the tree has two trunks that contrast with one another: one long, the other short; one bending downward, the other bending backward; one upright, the other slanting. The trunks should be arranged in such a way as to give variety to the shape of the tree. Depending upon difference in size, there can be grandfather-and-grandson, father-and-son, and brothers styles. The connecting point of the trunks will form an acute angle. Any species of trees may be used. Pots are chiefly square, rectangular, or oval.

Straight-line or raft style

A fallen tree's roots are partly broken when the trunk collapses; the existing branches continue to grow and become trunks which bear new roots. As time passes, the old and new roots become twisted together. These exposed and intertwined roots form a strikingly beautiful pattern. In this bonsai style, the distance between the trunks should vary, as should their thickness and height. The straight-line is a highly appealing style, very rich in variety. Any species can be used that is suitable for a rectangular or oval pot or a slab of rock.

Wind-swept style

Trees that grow on mountain tops, along the coast, or in windy regions have long been exposed to the force of strong winds from a single direction, so all their branches are swept to one side. The vigorous shape of the wind-swept tree can make the observer feel the kind of movement the tree experiences in its natural setting. The trunk may be of any thickness and height and may be slanting, bending, or stretching. The branches should grow in the direction the trunk leans. Old bonsai, withered branches, or one-sided branches can be used to create this style— a wonderful transformation of useless trees into precious bonsai. Suitable species are pine, Sargent juniper, needle juniper, and reef pemphis. Containers used are mainly round or rectangular pots or slabs of rocks.

Broom style

This charming style is one in which the tree looks like an upturned broom. Bonsai in this style should have a good root-base, a straight trunk, and fine and tender branches. Trees whose branches are bare in winter are particularly fascinating. The broom style can be further subdivided into full-broom, semi-broom, and twig-broom styles. Trees for this style usually grow on the plains. The Japanese gray-bark elm (zelkova) is a representative species. This style looks best in shallow, oval or rectangular pots.

A natural tree scene of branch tips gently interwoven.

A natural tree scene of meshed crossed roots.

A garden-style landscape.

Group planting, tray-landscape styles

Ordinary-looking trees of various heights and thicknesses can be planted in large, shallow pots or slabs of rock; and fine rocks, figurines, bridges, cottages, and boats may be added. Trees used in group plantings may be broken branches, one-sided branches, young trees, or even completely withered trees. This style allows the grower, in the shortest possible time, to make use of his creative techniques to fashion a work of art and natural beauty. The tray-landscape style has high appreciated value and is widely popular because it is rich in variety, the materials used are cheap, and production time is short. Furthermore, group plantings are very picturesque and naturally beautiful. Species used are common cryptomeria, Japanese black pine, Japanese grey-bark elm, Chinese hackberry, and Hinoki cypress. Rectangular or oval pots or flaky rocks should be chosen.

Clinging-to-a-rock, root-over-rock styles

Combining rocks with trees in bonsai more fully represents the beauty of nature and allows the artist to present different scenes, such as a sheer cliff, a ravine, or a rocky islet. The combination of trees and rocks must be harmonious and depict natural scenery in a realistic way.

Clinging-to-a-rock: In this style a tree is planted in the crevices of a rock, which serves as the pot. The roots attach to the rock and do not need soil to grow. The tree can be positioned on top or by the side of the rock. The bonsai is then arranged on a tray of water.

Root-over-rock: The roots of the tree cling to the rock and both are planted in a tray of soil. The upper portion of the roots is attached to the rock while the lower portion is planted in soil. Species of trees with long roots should be chosen for this style.

General guidelines for creating bonsai with rocks

(1) Choose a hard rock with textural variety. It should also have good water-absorbing capacity in order to provide moisture for the tree's growth.

(2) A short rock may be matched with all styles, but a tall rock harmonizes best with the cascade style.

(3) Select a tree that is slightly smaller than the rock so that when the tree grows, in three to five years, it will harmonize with the rock. This style looks artificial at first but will eventually have an aged feeling.

(4) Tropical varieties (such as Fukien tea and common jasmin orange) should be planted in summer, while ordinary species are normally planted in March before new buds appear. At that time of year, the weather becomes warmer and it is easier for trees to grow. The elm sprouts early so it can be planted in early spring. The pine and juniper can be planted in late fall or early winter.

Overhanging rocky cliffs with trees are often seen in Chinese landscape paintings.

A scene of dense tree growth in a natural setting.

曲成直難直程曲易
玩賞盆栽亦能悟得人生曲直之意也
悅美女史性喜盆栽熱心推廣歐閩其近
埋首著述中國盆栽藝術出書在即道中友輩莫不稱讚
歲次己巳 韓學田

The "upright" tree style.

138

平生多傲骨不畏雪霜寒
若待知音來隨開滿樹花
一九八九年夏月於古代堂
韓掃田

The ''slanting'' tree style.

何用別慶方外去
人間亦自有丹邱
悦真女史提句囑畫盆栽
一九八九年
韓錦田

The "coiled" tree style.

The "twisted-trunk" tree style.

141

勢如化龍入深淵 歲次己巳夏月韓錦田

The ''full cascade'' tree style.

嶺樹縣垂千里目江流曲似九迴腸 歲次己巳夏 李國安句 蒂錦田作圖

The "semi-cascade" tree style.

143

The "weeping" tree style.

一枝獨秀最惹騷人 歲次己巳夏夕 韓錦田

The "literati" tree style.

一聲南雁已先紅
莫炫他木耐深秋

一九八九年夏日
錦田

The "clump" tree style.

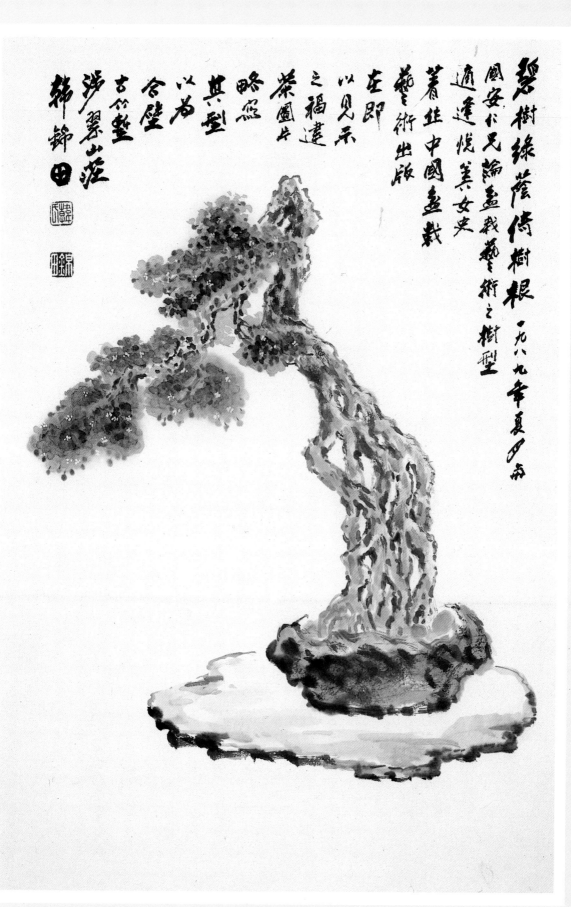

碧樹綠蔭倚樹根 一九八九年夏日於

國安代兄論盆栽藝術之樹型

適逢悅美女史

著並中國盆栽

藝術出版

在即

以見示

之福建

茶圖片

略窺

其型

以为

含璧

古竹莊

涉翠山莊

錦錦田

The "exposed-root" tree style.

蒸葉連峯合
巘巘石運涼
歲次己巳夏月
坐沙連幹榆
樹十餘牽荊
余嘗養一盂
韩讓台中仁坤
沈慶輝先生
不和如今樹容
可好
志竹塱
涉翠山莊
韩舒田

The "raft" tree style.

148

經年凌霜共艱苦
胎育一旦成化龍
歲次己巳
韓梓田

The "twin-trunk" tree style.

The "wind-swept" tree style.

沒有冬天的裸枝那來春天的嫩芽 一九八九年

歲次己巳夏 悅美女史絕句囑畫 古月堂 涉翠山莊 林錦田

The "broom" tree style.

151

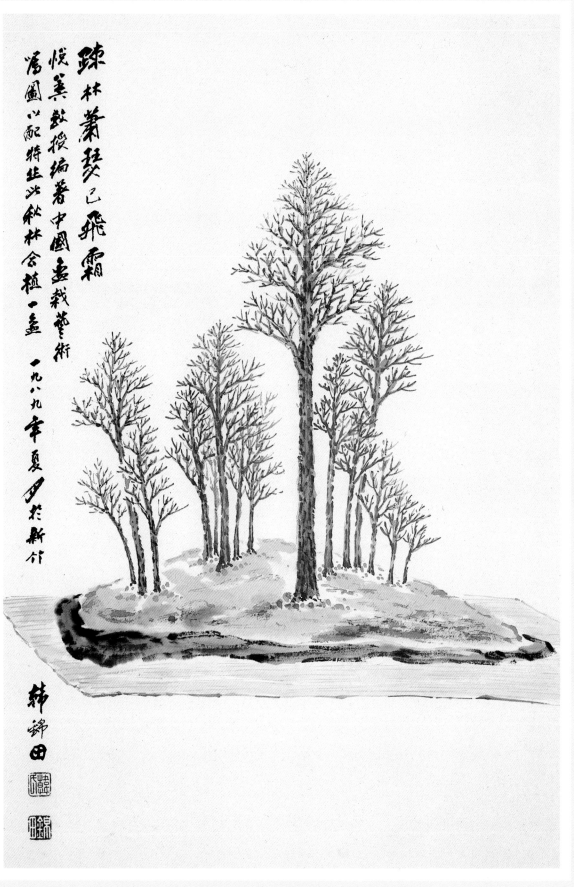

疎林蕭瑟已飛霜

悅美教授編著中國盆栽藝術

囑圖以配特植此秋林合植一盆

一九八九年夏于新竹

韓錦田

The "group planting" tree style.

152

真山安可仰徒此挹清蔈
悦美教授囑為畫栽松杏白勾題之歲次己巳於
新竹 韓錦田

The "root-over-rock" tree style.

GROUP PLANTING

A natural Taiwan hemlock forest.

Group Planting

Based on the example of scenery commonly found on mountains, hills, and plains or along streams, lakes, and seas, three or more trees may be planted together with fine rocks, ornaments, and grass on a wide container, a slab of rock, or a shuipan (watertray) to recreate the natural landscape in a realistic and three-dimensional way.

Characteristics of group planting

Group planting requires superior artistic wisdom and keen aesthetic judgment, and the artist must rely on his imagination to make an ingenious composition; therefore, this style best reveals the artist's creativity. Usually, a tree takes years of attentive care and cultivation to become a handsome bonsai, but group plantings can be finished in a short time, while satisfying the artist's creative impulses and providing great pleasure. This style also has endless variations and high aesthetic value. In addition, the materials used are relatively inexpensive. Among bonsai styles, group plantings may be said to be the most natural, realistic, and picturesque.

Group plantings are nearly-realistic presentations of the natural landscape. Trees of similar or different species, ages, styles, different heights and sizes or unhealthy trees, broken branches, one-sided branches, withered trees, and young trees may be arranged to create spatial variety. In a group planting, the artist attempts to convey the elegant atmosphere of the woodlands.

With this style, the artist can use the same materials to recreate a new setting or change the design every year or every few years, as he likes. The group planting is not only pleasing for the bonsai enthusiast but also provides him with an opportunity to perfect his horticultural techniques; it is, therefore, a good means for developing these techniques and making the art of bonsai more popular.

A natural "group-planting" scene.

A group planting bonsai decorating a window.

A Chinese hackberry in a forest-style group planting.

A Fukien tea tray-landscape bonsai.

A Chinese hackberry forest-style group planting.

A Japanese serissa tray-landscape bonsai.

Japanese gray-bark elm in a forest-style grouped planting.

Japanese gray-bark elm in a forest-style grouped planting.

Types of group planting

Forest-style group planting: Three or more trees are planted together to form a sparse grove or a dense forest. The design objective should be to emphasize unity and harmony with the materials arranged in an irregular triangle style. The arrangement of the bonsai can convey the impression of sparse woods or flourishing dense woods. The tree materials should be arranged according to different geographical environments. In general, conifers may be used to create a mountain forest scene where there is only a winding path but no ornament. Broad-leafed trees may be used to create a scene representing the plains or the hills, and, if needed, fine rocks or ornaments may be added.

Tray-landscape style group planting: This style best represents natural scenery. Trees, the dominant materials, are arranged with rocks, grasses, bridges, and figurines on a tray in agreeable patterns. The artist should be careful not to place all the ornaments together in one place; otherwise, the setting will look cluttered. The most important objective is to reveal a theme. Pebbles or moss can be used to embellish the scene. Fine sand or a narrow path between the trees can be arranged to convey the idea that the scene extends beyond the confines of the pot. In short, the objectives of creation are naturalism and realism. The artist should try to convey the atmosphere and mood of the countryside in order to achieve the aim of miniaturizing nature, displaying pleasing views of ''mountains and rivers contained in a tray,'' and to enjoy the ''delights of the woods in the house.''

Procedures for creating a group planting

(1) After deciding on the design, choose a suitable container. In order to make the landscape look magnificent and massive, a shallow, wide container of appropriate size should be selected. The container can be rectangular, oval, or irregular; or it can be a slab of rock. There are two types of containers, glazed and unglazed. For evergreens, choose black earthenware or nanman wares. For miscellaneous, flowering, and fruiting varieties, white glazed pots, celadon, or green glazed pots are preferable. Substitutes can be concrete pots or slabs of rock.

(2) Prepare trees of different heights and sizes. Never use trees of the same height in group plantings. The main tree must be tall and thick; the secondary trees and supplementary trees should be 3/4 and 2/3 the height of the main tree, respectively, and the supporting trees should be less than 1/2 the height of the main tree.

Rich green natural trees in a group planting scene.

A garden-type planted landscape.

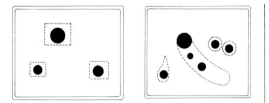

The basic layout of a group planting.

Stages in the creation of group planting (Trident maple):
(1) Prepared tools and plants.
(2) Moss prepared for arrangement on the bonsai soil surface.
(3) Soil for the inside of the container, contoured into irregular terrain.

Trees used in group plantings should be of similar species and have similar branches, foliage, bark, and age so that the design will be harmonious and unified. Try to prepare more trees than you need so that you have more choices when designing; the wider the variety of materials, the better the creation. In forest group plantings, it is best to make the main, secondary, and supplementary trees stand upright; if they are slanting, aluminum wire can be used to make them stand erect. Finally, it is best to choose tree materials with handsome surface roots. After all the tree materials are prepared, prune the branches and roots for use.

(3) Prepare the required rocks, moss, sphagnum moss, sand, clay, water, ornaments, and tools.

(4) Cover the drainage holes with plastic mesh and pass several wires through it to fix it in place. Add the soil mixture and sketch out divisions on the soil surface.

(5) In a forest setting, the main tree should be planted one-third to the right or left of center in the tray, secondary trees planted a little farther from it, and supplementary trees near it. Make sure that no two trees are in line or parallel each other. Whether viewed from above or frontally, the trees should form an irregular triangle; this is a fundamental guideline in creating group plantings.

In a jungle layout, there can be single, twin, or multiple jungle group plantings and various scenes can be created.

(6) Mix clay or shredded sphagnum moss with fine clay particles. Add water and stir them into a paste; then use the paste to form a rim around the edge of the pot. Next fill in with the soil mixture and landscape the soil surface; make sure that the soil surface is uneven to create perspective. Spread moss on top, and, if necessary, add ornaments.

Points to observe

(1) Do not arrange the materials at random. No two trees should be parallel with each other.

(2) Use shallow, wide containers and leave enough empty space to simulate the vastness of land.

(3) The thick focal tree and secondary tree should be planted in the front and short, small trees in the back. Trees on the right and the left should be arranged so that when viewed from the front and sides no tree conceals another. Try to arrange tree materials in such a way that they fully convey a view with perspective. Do not, however, arrange materials unnaturally.

(4) Trees in front should have branches that grow out from a higher place on the trunk, while those in the back should have branches that grow from a lower position. This arrangement creates perspective and three-dimensionality in a forest view.

(5) Rocks, trees, grass, and moss should be unified; also try to show the liveliness of seasonal changes in the composition.

(6) Rocks should have variety— preferably angles in order to simulate jutting rocks, islets, or crags. For fine rocks, choose those with pleasing color and texture, especially those that can retain moisture. It is also important that all rocks and trees be positioned in the same direction.

(7) It is ideal to have an odd number of trees in order to make the design look more lively and interesting. Try not to plant trees in the center of the container, to avoid making a dull-looking composition. (When the number of trees exceeds ten, this guideline does not apply.)

(8) The roots of trees in group plantings should be near the edges of the container so that they receive sufficient sunlight and absorb fresh air to maintain healthy growth.

All in all, the creation of a group planting should be characterized by unity in design and should show that each element in the group is closely related to the others but retains its individual characteristics. The purpose is to have every tree and every leaf tell the story of its life in a natural setting.

Guidelines for soil change in group plantings

(1) Remove the trees. Because the roots will be linked together, use a bamboo stick to remove the earth on first the lower and then the upper parts. It is important not to damage the roots.

(2) In order to maintain the shape of a group planting, change only half the soil. Soil can be totally changed, but every tree must then be replanted individually.

(3) If trees must be encouraged to grow wider, use coarser soil in the soil change; if the original size must be maintained, use thinner soil.

(4) During repotting, the long roots of trees in the center must be pulled out to the pot rim to allow them to grow well and receive sufficient sunshine and water. This will prevent the roots from withering and growing unhealthy.

(5) Apply fertilizers to the new soil one month after the soil change.

(4) Trees are planted in each level of terrain.
(5) The completed arrangement of the bonsai soil surface.
(6) The completed group planting creation.

Elegant stones and green moss decorate the group planting.

163

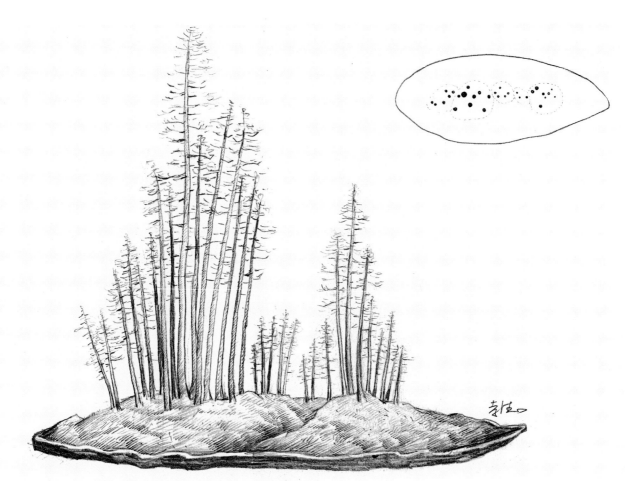

A dense forest scene (31 paired Chinese hackberry in a group planting).

A dispersed forest scene (13 Japanese gray-bark elms in a group planting).

164

A peninsular scene (a single pine tree tray-landscape planting).

A coastal scene (tray-landscape planted with 5 black pines).

A river bed scene (tray-landscape planted with 9 fir trees).

A lake scene (tray-landscape planted with 3 weeping willows).

Luxuriant forest scene (planted with 41 maples in three groups).

Solitary island scene (a single pine tree tray-landscape planting).

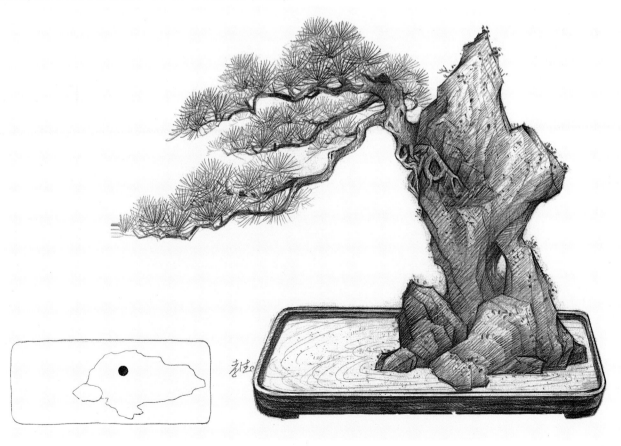

PLANT PHYSIOLOGY

A tall tree resting on a large root network in a natural setting.

Plant Physiology

The plant is a kind of living organism. In temperatures above 50°F and below 86°F, it engages in the growth activities of absorption, synthesis, assimilation, and secretion. A plant grows most actively in a temperature range of 68°F to 77°F and relative humidity between 70% and 90%. Due to the limitations of the amount of soil in the pot, the roots of a bonsai cannot extend as freely as they can in nature. The bonsai also lacks a natural water source, and it is necessary to prune and pick a bonsai regularly; therefore, sunshine, air, water and soil requirements become particularly important. It is imperative to understand the biological functions of the plant to make correct judgments about the growth process. This allows the bonsai creator to choose the correct times perform the work that is necessary to achieve the desired design.

Functions of roots

The growth of the roots begins in the meristematic tissue behind the root cap. Roots grow all night long (in the daytime, because of sunshine, the growth process is very slow), and after two or three weeks, they begin to age. Root hair and epidermal cells absorb water and nutrients which are conducted up the xylem (tracheae or vessel members) to the leaves, but a great deal of water (about 97%) is given up to the air during the process that is known as transpiration.

It is believed that the rise of water in the plant body is caused by (1) root pressure, (2) capillary action, (3) transpiration, and (4) cohesion. Thus, if the soil in the pot is too dry, root hair will wither and be unable to absorb water and inorganic nutrients. If the soil is too wet, the roots will suffocate and decay, losing their absorbing capacity. In these instances, as water vapors continue to evaporate from the leaf surface, the tree may finally die of dehydration. Roots provide absorption, storage, and excretion for the plant. They discharge heavy inorganic salt secretions left by the plant. Roots also serve as a kind of anchor for the plant. For the purpose of fixing the plant, the roots of a plant penetrate into the soil and are closely connected, holding the plant firmly in place and giving it stability.

Plants cannot make use of nitrogen in the air directly; but some bacteria, like mycorrhiza, make their way into the roots of living plants and fix nitrogen between the soil particles for the use of the plant. These bacteria have a symbiotic relationship with the plant and obtain their food from the plant. For the roots to grow well, an abundant amount of aqueous vapor is necessary. Normally, roots grow along the inner edge of the pot downward. Because water usually gathers around the edge of the pot, the temperature there is higher and thus the roots grow more. It is, however, important that the soil not be too wet because fresh air must be able to enter the pot; oxygen is necessary to improve the growth of the roots. Thus, water, air, sunshine, and temperature must be carefully monitored in bonsai cultivation.

A tree growing on the surface of a rock becomes more rigid as the thick root growth heads downward.

Functions of the trunk, branches, and skin

The trunk and branches support the weight of the tree and are the main elements in building a beautiful shape in the plant. The skin protects the interior part of the plant; the vessels provide channels for the passage of nutrition to the leaves and branches. These vessels are the means by which water and nutrition absorbed by roots are passed to the leaves. Vigorous cell division makes the trunk grow. The wooden section supports the tree. The age of the tree can be determined from the annual ring.

Functions of leaves

Photosynthesis

Leaves are the place where the tree processes food and absorbs and transpires water.

Leaves of green plants use light energy to perform photosynthesis. In the daytime, within the chloroplasts in the mesophyll cells, water transported from the roots combines with carbon dioxide assimilated through stomata on the leaf surface to form glucose (carbohydrate), which supplies the plant with the nutrition and energy necessary for growth. At the same time, oxygen is released, renewing the air human beings and animals breathe. The process of photosynthesis may be simplified as follows:

$$6\ H_2O + 6\ CO_2 \xrightarrow[\text{chloroplasts}]{\text{sunlight}} C_6H_{12}O_6 + 6\ O_2 \uparrow$$

water | carbon dioxide | glucose (carbohydrates) | oxygen

Green plants are the only "factories" that can effectively capture light energy, which is then converted into chemical energy and stored in carbohydrates. Other organisms on earth, like animals, fungi, and bacteria, depend on carbohydrates manufactured by plants for the maintenance of life.

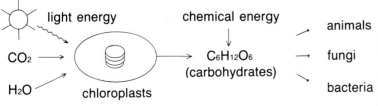

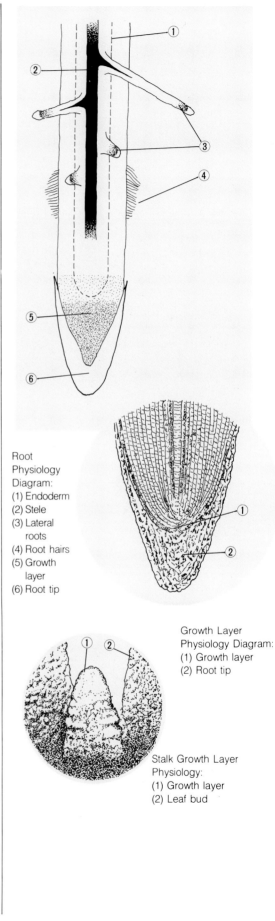

Root Physiology Diagram:
(1) Endoderm
(2) Stele
(3) Lateral roots
(4) Root hairs
(5) Growth layer
(6) Root tip

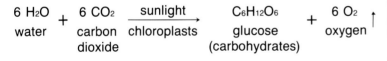

Growth Layer Physiology Diagram:
(1) Growth layer
(2) Root tip

Stalk Growth Layer Physiology:
(1) Growth layer
(2) Leaf bud

171

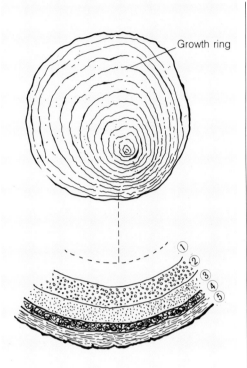

Tree Trunk Cross-Sectional Diagram:
(1) Xylem
(2) Vessels area
(3) Cambium
(4) Sieve tubes area
(5) Cortex

Plant Growth Circulation

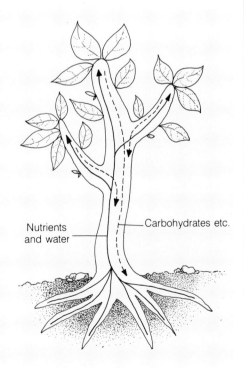

Large quantities of carbohydrates are produced through photosynthesis. Besides providing material for cell metabolism, carbohydrates are temporarily stored in leaves during the daytime. At night, they are translocated by sieve tubes (sieve tube members) in the phloem to roots, branches, flowers, and fruits for growth and storage.

Cells containing chloroplasts perform photosynthesis very efficiently. An estimated 170 billion tons of carbon dioxide can be fixed (synthesized) and converted into organic compounds in one year. At present, there are about 700 billion tons of carbon dioxide in the atmosphere. Every year, over 1/5 of it can be converted into biological compounds through photosynthesis. Of course, this does not mean that, once fixed, carbon dioxide will disappear from the atmosphere forever; carbon dioxide is released back into the atmosphere during the respiratory process of animals and human beings. Moreover, the widespread usage of carbonic fuels (petroleum and coal) also accounts for the return of carbon dioxide to the atmosphere.

In recent years, many forests and grasslands have been destroyed through the increasing demands of mankind. As a result, the amount of carbon dioxide fixed and oxygen released by plants have decreased markedly, and quality of the air has deteriorated correspondingly. In cities, especially, the number of concrete buildings, cars, and factories are increasing rapidly. Our lives seem to be more comfortable; but, in reality, the most basic conditions of our existence—clean air and water—are threatened as they have never been before in human history.

Although the Environmental Protection Administration makes repeated warnings about serious air pollution, it is a dangerous problem that remains unsolved. Therefore, the growing of green plants is more than an enjoyable but dispensable hobby; our very survival depends on it.

Transpiration

Water evaporates more quickly in broad-leafed trees than in conifers. Generally, the rate of evaporation varies with the humidity of the air. If the air is dry, evaporation occurs more quickly, whereas evaporation is slower if the air is moist. The process of transpiration is chiefly carried out by the stomata or air pores on the underside of the leaves, but some water vapor is also lost through the cuticles of the leaves.

Nearly all plants possess the characteristic of absorbing water and minerals (inorganic salts) through the leaf surface. Conifers usually have a greater capacity to absorb water than broad-leafed trees. Even though the amount of water absorbed by the leaves is not sufficient for growth, it can still maintain a minimal life mechanism in the plant. In the case of root decay, transplanting, or serious root damage in a conifer, water must be sprayed on the leaf surface; this will supply the conifer with water for absorption. In the case of broad-leafed trees, spraying water helps prevent the evaporation of water from the leaf surface. Broad-leafed trees do not need spraying when they are transplanted after their leaves fall.

Respiration

Photosynthesis is production, and respiration is consumption. Energy required to maintain the plant's life is produced by means of respiration, a catabolic process in which glucose (carbohydrate) produced in photosynthesis is oxidized and broken down into simpler inorganic substances (carbon dioxide and water) and stored chemical energy released. This chemical energy can then be used to do "work"— for instance, promoting the growth process and synthesizing glucose produced in photosynthesis into starch, which is the stored energy of plants. Most people think that respiration in trees takes place only on the leaf surface. In fact, there are a few air pores, or lenticels, on the surface of roots, trunks, stems, and branches where gaseous exchange also takes place to supply the cells with oxygen for respiration.

The respiration process is completely different from photosynthesis. Living cells in plants perform respiration day and night. The process can be simplified as follows:

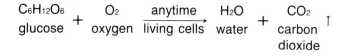

$$C_6H_{12}O_6 \text{ (glucose)} + O_2 \text{ (oxygen)} \xrightarrow[\text{living cells}]{\text{anytime}} H_2O \text{ (water)} + CO_2 \text{ (carbon dioxide)} \uparrow$$

Because roots are buried beneath the earth surface and, as such, are unaffected by sunlight, they are constantly carrying out respiration—taking in oxygen and releasing carbon dioxide; as a result, carbonic acid is readily formed in the soil, making it acid. Oxygen causes bacteria to decompose dead organic matter in the soil, converting it into inorganic mineral salts for absorption by the roots. Therefore, keeping the soil well aerated and using granular soil in planting have considerable influence on the proper growth and absorption capacity of the roots as well as on the overall shape and vigor of the tree. The rate of photosynthesis in the leaves is directly proportional to the absorptive capacity of the roots.

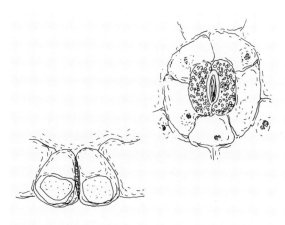

Stoma Section Diagram:
(1) Side view of the closing of the stoma.
(2) Cross-sectional view of an opened stoma.

Plants need light to thrive and flourish.

173

1

Seasonal changes

Because a bonsai must adjust to seasonal changes in temperature and humidity, the condition of its growth also varies with the seasons. When the temperature and humidity are high, the rate of photosynthesis speeds up; it slows down when the temperature and humidity are low. When a bonsai is being trained, the physiological state of the tree's growth in each season must be taken into consideration. A bonsai grower must never attempt to work counter to the physiology of the plant. For instance, transplanting, repotting, pruning, or training bonsai on a hot summer day can cause the tree to wither and die or undergo abnormal growth (tropical varieties are exceptions) due to the functions of absorption and transpiration. Thus, for creating a bonsai with a perfect shape, it is necessary to understand the tree's biological conditions thoroughly. In spring, before budding, the plant is still in semi-hibernation. Use this time to remove and change the soil and wind wires to train the shape of bonsai. Use the summer to do the work of picking and pruning; and, in fall, fertilize the bonsai to prepare for the coming winter. In winter, take measures to help the bonsai resist cold temperatures.

The general growth cycle of deciduous plants

Growth Cycle	Hibernation Period		Nourishment Growth Period			Reproduction and Growth Period		Nutrition Accumulation Period		Hibernation Period
Month	1	2	3	4	5	6	7	8	9	10	11	12

Seasonal Changes of Deciduous Trees (Japanese red maple)
(1) Changing color to deep red at the onset of autumn.
(2) Naked branches after leaves drop off for winter.
(3) The green leaves of spring and summer.

GUIDELINES FOR BONSAI CULTIVATION

Bonsai soil structure (fine soil on the top, coarse soil on the bottom).

Guidelines for Bonsai Cultivation

The necessary elements for bonsai growth include (A) soil, (B) sunlight and placement, (C) watering, (D) fertilization, and (E) control of pests and diseases. A detailed discussion is as follows:

Soil

Soil is formed from weathered rocks. It provides plants with the minerals and water necessary for growth and is also a medium to which roots cling for support and stability. Soil is, therefore, an extremely important element in the vegetative environment.

Soil is composed of a complex interactive system of solids (inorganic minerals, organic matters), liquids (water), and gases (air). The solid form of soil, which is composed of grains of various shapes and sizes, is called the soil texture (e.g. sand, silt, and clay); the combination or arrangement of soil particles is called the soil structure (e.g. single-grained structure, crumb structure).

The difference in texture and structure determines the physical properties of soil. For example, the amount of space (pores) between soil particles can influence drainage, water retention, aeration, nutrition-supplying capacity, aggregation, and spread of the root system.

Bonsai soil

Soil used to grow bonsai is called bonsai soil. Bonsai soil is equivalent to plant food, and its quality can directly affect the growth of the tree. Good bonsai soil should have the following characteristics:

High water-retaining and nutrition-absorbing capacity: After the fine sand has been sifted out, half-weathered granular soil with a crumb structure is full of capillaries, which allow it to absorb water easily. This type of soil retains water sufficient to dissolve inorganic nutrition for absorption by the roots. After fertilization, the soil is able to retain most of the nutritive elements.

Good drainage: If the soil is composed of very fine particles and the space between soil particles is small, root decay will occur due to poor ventilation as well as poor drainage.

Moderate pH level: Depending upon the species of the tree, choose a bonsai soil— slightly acid or alkaline (pH 6 – 7.5)— that is most favorable for the tree's growth.

Granular soil with crumb structure: This type of soil has large pore spaces, good drainage, high nutrition-absorbing capacity, and good ventilation. In well-ventilated soil, roots grow easily and bacteria can process nutrition quickly to protect the soil from becoming acidified.

Fresh soil with pleasing appearance and color: The soil on the earth's surface contains both organic and inorganic minerals, but most of its contents are used up by plants or washed away by rain. Therefore, about one yard below the earth's surface lies half-weathered fresh soil that contains more minerals and has better appearance and color. Using this soil in potting a bonsai not only ensures better growth but also enhances the beauty of the tree.

The three interacting elements of soil consistency: soil particles are the large dotted cells, water is denoted by the contiguous black network, and ventilating air is indicated by the unmarked cells.

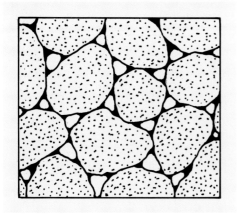

Preparing bonsai soil and controlling bonsai growth

The amount of water required by plants varies from one type to another, as do soil requirements. The pine and juniper need sufficient water but should not be overwatered. Because these varieties need to display strength and ruggedness, it is better to use mixed soil with a high percentage of sand. Because miscellaneous varieties, flowering and fruiting varieties, and herbs have a luxuriant growth of branchlets, flowers, and fruit, a loamy soil with a high capacity for retaining water and absorbing fertilizers should be used.

Half-finished bonsai require coarse soil so that the roots can thicken more easily and the trunk and branches grow faster. Established bonsai should, however, be grown in soil with finer particles to maintain the shape of the trees. Large soil particles should be used as bottom soil in big and deep containers, whereas finer soil particles should be used in small and shallow containers. When mixing a soil, pay attention to the amount of moisture, air, and fertilizer required by the tree in order to control growth and improve quality.

Types and characteristics of bonsai soil

Mountain sand: The grains are small and angular. Mountain sand has large soil pores and excellent drainage. When mixed with red clay, it helps prevent soil hardening. It can also help tap roots send out fine lateral roots.

River sand: This soil is finer than mountain sand. Its hardness is between that of rock and clay. It has fair water retentivity and good drainage but contains fewer inorganic minerals and organic materials.

Clay: This soil is very sticky and used in brickmaking. In creating a rock planting, clay can be used to bind the roots in place. It helps induce flower growth and prevents the falling of fruit when mixed in a fruit tree medium.

Weathered rocks: Weathered rocks are very hard and provide excellent drainage. When placed at the bottom of the pot, they can regulate the amount of moisture in the soil.

Humus: This soil is formed from decayed dead leaves and manure that has become thoroughly fermented after two or three years. Because humus contains bacteria and worm eggs, it is safer to sterilize the soil in hot wind or the sun's ultraviolet rays before using. Humus has a large capacity to retain water and a rich reserve of organic nutrients and microbes; these loosen the soil and improve ventilation, helping to prevent the soil from becoming acidic. Thus, humus can be used as a base fertilizer for flowering and fruiting varieties.

Red clay: This brownish red soil is formed from weathered igneous rocks. Its hardness is between that of sand and clay. When it is wet, it becomes sticky and does not dissolve easily. When it is dry, it is hard to break. It has large capillary pores, a large capacity for retaining water, good drainage ability, and good ventilating ability. Despite having few nutritive elements, it absorbs water and fertilizers readily. When mixed with sand, it is the most important soil used in bonsai cultivation. Yangmingshan and Tatushan (two mountains in Taiwan) have red clay soil.

Organic material (humus).

Weathered rocks.

River sand.

Red clay granules.

179

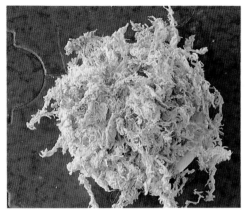

Sphagnum moss is the best material for covering wounds and retaining moisture.

Bonsai on raised platforms in a garden.

Miniature bonsai placed together on a shelf.

Sphagnum moss: This is a type of aquatic plant growing in rivers or marshes. Because sphagnum moss resists bacteria and decay and possesses a large capacity to absorb water, it was used as a wound dressing during World War I. In horticulture, it is used as a wound dressing and wrapping material. Sphagnum moss is also used to cover the soil surface to keep moisture in and prevent drying or rotting after transplanting and repotting.

Sunlight and placement

When you are choosing a position for your bonsai, it is important to consider the conditions of sunlight, ventilation, fresh air, and nightdew. The bonsai's source of energy is sunlight. In sunshine, a bonsai absorbs carbon dioxide to manufacture carbohydrates. Because photosynthesis influences the growth of bonsai, it is essential to expose the tree to sunlight for at least five hours a day to allow it to perform photosynthesis. However, avoid putting the tree under the scorching afternoon sun. It is preferable to expose the bonsai to the warm and gentle morning sun. Also, remember to adjust the position of the tree every week to ensure balanced growth on all sides.

The ideal position for a bonsai has good ventilation and sufficient sunlight. Daily changes in temperature and intensity of sunlight should be carefully considered. Avoid direct and intense sunlight. When temperatures rise beyond the critical limit, the rate of photosynthesis will slow down and the roots will stop functioning. This will cause the leaves to become scorched and the soil to dry up.

In general, miscellaneous varieties are particularly vulnerable to strong sunshine and are most likely to suffer from loss of vigor, leaf burn, wilting, and dehydration. Insufficient sunshine may also cause the growth of long internodes, which weaken tree growth. Finally, the bonsai should also be protected against typhoons and wintry winds.

The height of a bonsai stand is usually about 24 in.; this is a convenient and comfortable height for the control and appreciation of bonsai. Do not put the bonsai directly on the ground because ants, earthworms, and snails may attack the tree through the drainage holes in the bottom of the pot. Fine roots may also creep into the ground, weakening the root-base and distorting the overall design. Neither is it correct to put the bonsai directly on the cement floor of a roof garden because a bonsai is easily weakened in a high-temperature and dry environment.

Never place a bonsai near an exhaust outlet. Do not put a bonsai in an air-conditioned or heated room for more than one day or keep it indoors for more than three days.

Watering

Water is the major component of plants and constitutes about 70% of their makeup. It is one of the most important conditions for plant growth. A thorough knowledge of watering is, therefore, essential to bonsai cultivation. Watering the bonsai may seem to be very simple but in reality is not. The amount of water needed varies and is dependent upon the weather, the species, and condition of the tree, the state of the soil, and the position of the tree. To give the tree the right amount of water to match its daily requirements is not easy and is certainly beyond the ability of the layman. Beginners usually have to practice watering for at least three years in order to understand and be able to control it. A common expression among bonsai enthusiasts is, ''It takes three years to learn to water a tree properly.''

Too much water and over-frequent watering will cause abnormal elongation of the internodes of the tree, which weakens the density of the tree and makes the overall design shaggy. If the soil is poorly drained, overwatering will cause root decay. But if the amount of water given is inadequate, the tree will wither up and die. Generally speaking, the proper way to supply water is to water the tree in the morning and around four in the afternoon, then dig 1/2 in. deep into the soil to see if it is still moist. If the soil is moist, the amount of water is correct.

When good bonsai soil is dry, its pore spaces will be filled with air. Because roots absorb carbon dioxide from the soil air and release oxygen during respiration, the carbon dioxide of the soil becomes higher and may damage the growth of the roots. Watering the soil can help to push out old soil air and draw in fresh air as water drains through the bottom holes. Therefore, alternating dryness and dampness of the soil is essential to balance the proportions of soil, water, and oxygen.

Watering methods

The principle of watering bonsai is to fill the pot with water with one watering until extra water drains away through the drainage holes. If the soil does not become saturated with one watering, the grower should try to find out whether it is due to poor absorbing capacity of the soil or because the roots have filled the pot, necessitating immediate transplanting and repotting.

Pay attention to the watering of bonsai during the drizzling rain season.
When sprinkling bonsai, be sure that the flow is downward and vertical to cleanse the leaves.

Bonsai must be watered daily without fail.

Using a sprayer to water bonsai.

181

Water is an indispensable element of plant growth.

If the drainage of a bonsai is adequate, water should flow freely from the bottom of the container, as pictured.

During the rainy season, bonsai containers should be propped up on one side for better drainage.

In spring, summer, and fall, watering should be done twice daily. The optimum times for watering are from seven to eight in the morning and four to five in the afternoon. In summer, when the night temperature is high, the tree continues to perform respiration speedily; therefore, it is necessary to sprinkle the leaves between eight and nine. When the weather is cold in winter, it is enough to water the tree once a day or once every two days. Try to keep the soil dry throughout the night in winter because the pot temperature will be higher. If the temperature of the soil, air, and water is below 59°F, the activity of the roots will be impeded; if the temperature is even lower and the soil is damp, the soil will freeze and the roots are likely to be damaged. It is, therefore, necessary to pay constant attention to changes in temperatures and humidity.

After several days of continual heavy rainfall, one side of the pot should be tilted to speed up drainage to prevent root decay. After a shower or drizzle, only the surface soil is moist, so the tree will still need sufficient watering. Because of air pollution, rainwater is often acid; it is, therefore, necessary to wash the leaves thoroughly after every rainfall.

In midsummer, the pot soil becomes very dry at noon, and the sprouts and young shoots will droop due to loss of water; it is then necessary to water the tree immediately. In the past, it was believed that watering the plant at noon on a hot summer day, when the soil temperature was high, might scald the roots. In truth, the evaporation of water after watering can help to reduce the temperature of the soil. It was also said that water could scorch leaves because it was able to collect and reflect sunlight. This is also groundless. If sunlight goes through a drop of dew completely, its energy is only 0.2 calorie per minute. It is, therefore, incapable of burning leaves. Water evaporates quickly under the hot sun. The greater the area of the pot, the faster the rate of evaporation. Water will first evaporate before becoming hot. In addition, 1/4 oz. of water absorbs approximately 540 calories of heat when it evaporates; it is clear that instead of scorching the leaves, water helps lower temperature. Burning of leaves is caused by neither reflection of water nor heated water but by dehydration. Based on the author's experimentation over many years, watering and cleaning leaves in a room temperature above 74°F in midsummer will not hinder a tree's growth; rather, it will improve growth. In fact, temperature reaches its highest level at around three in the afternoon. Watering the soil at midday on a hot summer day can help lower the temperature of the soil in the pot. Because transpiration is rapid on the leaf surface, a supply of water at the right time is not harmful but helpful to bonsai.

The tree needs a greater amount of water during germination in spring and its flourishing period in summer. Once a week, the grower can practice immersion: the bonsai is put in a basin of water to soak until air bubbles cease coming through the soil. This method allows the tree to absorb sufficient water and helps to strengthen its growth. From the duration of bubbling, the bonsai grower can judge whether or not the bonsai is rootbound and requires repotting. When a bonsai is lacking water, its leaves will fall to resist evaporation. This phenomenon is an obvious sign of water insufficiency.

After winter dormancy, leaf pruning, or repotting, the tree does not need much water. This is especially true after repotting because the roots of the bonsai have not yet developed. For a newly repotted bonsai, spray the foliage in the daytime to provide extra water; and, unless the soil has become dry, refrain from watering the tree in the afternoon. This will keep the soil dry to raise the soil temperature. Because roots keep on growing throughout the night, this method can be used to induce the tree to root.

In flowering and fruiting varieties, flower buds need water when they swell. Do not cut off the water supply, or else the petals will not open fully, and the flowers will be poor and ugly. When the tree blossoms, water the soil directly but avoid watering the petals or they may decay. A sprayer with a very fine mouth may be used to sprinkle the leaves from bottom to top twice a day. This will help prolong the life span of the flowers and increase the rate of pollination and fertilization.

A tree absorbs water through its leaf surface as well as through its roots. It is, therefore, preferable to use a spray with a fine mouth and sprinkle the tree from the apex to wash away the dust and dirt in the lenticels and cuticles. Then water the tree in an upward movement from bottom to top to wash away worm eggs and allow the leaves to absorb moisture. This method of watering achieves better results, because the underside of leaves has a high water-absorbing capacity.

Emergency treatment for wilting

The most important part of the daily care of bonsai, watering, demands patience. Negligence in this task can cause the drooping of sprouts and young shoots and damage to the root cap and root hair. When a tree is slightly damaged, water it more frequently, and it will soon recover. For severe damage, put the bonsai in a large basin of water for three to four hours. After the soil has absorbed sufficient water, move the tree to a cool, shady place. Let it stand for two or three days and sprinkle the leaves daily until the roots and leaves recover their normal functions. For more serious damage, immediate leaf pruning and repotting is necessary. The withered roots must be pruned and the cuts wrapped with sphagnum moss. Water the leaves and put the tree in a damp place that is not windy. There is no other way to restore the tree.

Some people bury miniature bonsai with their pots or place bonsai on the ground to lower pot temperature and reduce the amount of water. If this method is used, the bottom of the pot must be examined every fifteen days to see if roots are growing out of the drainage holes. If they are, remove them immediately; otherwise, when vigorous roots are formed, the roots in the pot will quickly weaken and age, losing their absorbing capacity. With the formation of vigorous roots, spindling branches also develop, resulting in the subsequent wilting of weakened roots and loss of branches. It is advisable to place bonsai on the ground only when taking a short vacation. Otherwise, this method of cultivation makes it relatively difficult to create a handsome root-base.

How to aid the recovery of a withered plant (Nagasaki crab-apple):
(1) When the leaves of a bonsai droop from lack of water, the container must be partially submersed in water immediately.
(2) Following initial recovery, the bonsai plant will be in fragile condition and should be placed in a shady area.

Fertilization is necessary to provide the growing bonsai with additional nutrition.

Use plastic containers over solid fertilizers to prevent scattering.

Solid fertilizers can also be secured to the bonsai container with metal wire.

The main components of fertilizers

Fertilizers	Nitrogen (N)	Phosphorus (P)	Potassium (K)	Effects
Vegetable dregs	5.7	2.9	1.5	Slow
Sesame oil dregs	7.1	3.3	1.3	Slow
Rice bran	2.0	3.3	1.3	Slow
Fish meal	7.7	9.2	- - -	Slow
Bone meal	4.0	22.0	- - -	Slow
Tree & grass ashes	- - -	3.0	7.0	Slow
Hyponex	6.5	6.0	19.0	Rapid
Urea	47.0	- - -	- - -	Rapid
Superphosphate	- - -	20.5	- - -	Rapid
Potassium sulfate	- - -	- - -	50.0	Slow

The components of fertilizers and the symptoms of insufficiency or superfluity

Components	Symptoms of insufficiency or superfluity
Nitrogen(N)	Insufficiency of N will cause weakening of plants, inadequate greening of treetops, yellowing of tree bottoms, and, in serious cases, falling and withering of leaves. Too much N will cause overgrowth of branches, which is also harmful to bonsai.
Phosphorus(P)	Insufficiency of P will retard root growth and tend to retard the growth of the whole plant. Leaf color will change from turbid deep green to bronze and then purple.
Potassium(K)	The symptoms of K insufficiency are not obvious. When K is severely lacking, old leaves will show symptoms first: the tips or the edges of leaves will form dots or yellow spots then turn brown or red-brown, simulating leaf burn.
Minor elements	With a lack of ferrum and manganese, new leaves will turn yellow or white; with a lack of magnesium, the lower parts of leaves toward the top of a tree will turn yellow or red.

Fertilization

Understanding the needs of bonsai in using supplementary fertilizers

A bonsai is grown in a limited amount of soil within the confines of a pot. Organic materials available in the soil are constantly dissolved by bacteria into usable inorganic salts for absorption by the roots. As the tree grows, these essential nutrients in the soil become fewer and eventually fail to meet the requirements of the tree. Thus fertilization is necessary to provide the tree with additional nutrition.

Before fertilizing the tree, the grower must have a thorough knowledge of the growth stages of the tree and the amount of fertilizers required in order to apply them efficiently. The correct time for fertilization varies with the species, age, and placement of the bonsai as well as the nature of the fertilizers used. The grower must understand the growth, distribution, and absorbing capacity of the roots before deciding on the kind of fertilizers to be used. Fertilizers can produce the best possible effects if applied at the most appropriate place. Normally, young growing trees and food-storing trees require frequent fertilizing, but old established bonsai and dormant trees need less.

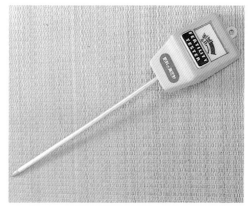

A soil fertility tester.

The rate of utilization

Not all of the fertilizers applied to bonsai soil can be fully absorbed and utilized by the tree; some are lost through evaporation, some during decomposition; others drain away through holes in the pot bottom during daily watering.

The rate of fertilizer absorption according to different methods is as follows:

Applying to soil: Nitrogen, 50% – 70%; phosphorus, 45%; and potassium, 40% – 50%.

Spraying on leaves: Nitrogen, 95%; phosphorus, 54%; and potassium, 80%.

Bonsai require only a small amount of liquid fertilizer when it is sprayed on leaves, and the effects are more rapid. Because the cuticle layer and stomata of leaves are also capable of absorbing fertilizer, applying fertilizer to the leaves directly accelerates the process of photosynthesis. An increased rate of photosynthesis and a rich supply of organic nutrition make the roots more active and able to absorb more water and nutrition. As a result, the metabolic process of the overall tree is improved. However, if this method of fertilizing is continued for a long period of time, the roots of the tree may weaken and degenerate. Therefore, leaf spraying should be alternated with soil applications of fertilizer.

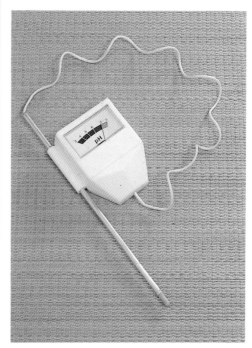

A pH meter for measuring acidity and alkalinity.

The four essential elements of fertilizers

Fertilizers are substances that supply plants with minerals. Plants are largely (92% – 95%) composed of carbon, hydrogen, and oxygen. The remaining 5% – 8% is made up of 13 necessary elements. Six of them are required in greater quantities and are known as macroelements, namely, nitrogen (N), phosphorus (P), potassium (K), calcium (Ca), sulphur (S), and magnesium (Mg). The remaining seven, which are needed in smaller quantities, are named microelements: manganese (Mn), iron (Fe), copper (Cu), boron (B), molybdenum (Mo), zinc (Zn), and chlorine (Cl).

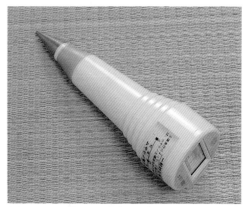

A hygrometer for measuring soil humidity.

Urea.

Potassium chloride.

Superphosphate lime.

Usually, fertilization refers to the application of nitrogen, phosphorus, potassium, and calcium.

Nitrogen (N): This element is an important component of protein, which constitutes the nuclei of live cells. Without protein, no creature can live. An insufficiency of nitrogen will reduce the green color of the leaves and weaken reproductive ability. Too much nitrogen will wither stems and leaves. Because it functions to produce leaf tissue, proteins, and hormones to make leaves flourish, nitrogen is called the "leaf fertilizer."

Phosphorus (P): This element is important for cell formation and division. When applied with nitrogen and potassium, phosphorus becomes very active. An excess of phosphorus won't hurt the plant, but a deficiency will affect the growth of the roots. Phosphorus fertilizer is primarily made from bone meal. When fruit bonsai is repotted, bone meal is usually put on the bottom of the pot or scattered on the soil surface. Because phosphorus helps the trees produce blossoms and fruit, it is called the "flower fertilizer" or "fruit fertilizer."

Potassium (K): Potassium has great influence on photosynthesis. It increases the transport of nutrition to roots and branches to make them expand actively. Potassium can also adjust a soil that is too acid and change the acidity of soil made from tree and grass ashes, which contain 60% potassium. Furthermore, potassium helps strengthen roots, aids in the absorption of nitrogen and phosphorus, and increases resistance to coldness and heat. It is thus called the "root fertilizer."

Calcium (Ca): Besides aiding plant growth and metabolism, calcium helps prevent solidification of soil and promotes nitrogen fixation by bacteria.

Classification of fertilizers

According to the way they are formulated, fertilizers can be classified into chemically synthesized inorganic fertilizers and natural organic fertilizers. Inorganic fertilizers are highly concentrated and have a stable composition; long-term application of inorganic fertilizers can easily acidify or alkalize the pot soil, impeding plant growth. When using a urea solution in rainy areas, it is better to dilute the solution using 1% urea to 1000% water and spray the solution directly on the leaf surface in the evening, especially when the Sargent juniper changes the shape of its leaves in March and September. Organic fertilizers in the soil are decomposed by bacteria into water-soluble inorganic salts, which are then slowly absorbed by the roots. Organic fertilizers are often applied in spring and fall. Since only a limited amount of soil is used in growing a bonsai, it is safer to use diluted organic fertilizers as they do not easily cause overfertilization.

There are two methods of fertilization: pre-repotting fertilizing and in-growth fertilizing. Pre-repotting fertilizing is used to promote the development of flowers and fruit in flowering and fruiting varieties. Prior to repotting, bone meal or leaf mold is mixed into the soil. Fertilizers that are applied to soil before planting must be completely fermented because, if they ferment in the pot, the heat generated can burn the roots. The in-growth fertilizing method is to apply fertilizers to the pot soil or the leaves of a growing tree. Because pre-repotting fertilizing is likely to encourage the attack of pests in the soil that are difficult to detect, it is better to use in-growth fertilizing.

Forms of fertilizers

Fertilizers come in both soild and liquid forms.

Application and formulation of organic liquid fertilizers

In proportions of 7 parts of oil dreg to 3 parts of bone meal, organic liquid fertilizer should be mixed in water ten times its volume. Allow the solution to ferment completely and then further dilute it by adding more water to ten times its volume. The apply the solution to the pot soil. If you cannot stand the offensive smell of this fertilizer, you can add sulfuric acid to it. Besides eliminating the offensive smell, sulfuric acid also gives the leaves a bright green color and reduces black pigmentation.

Application and formulation of solid fertilizers

The most common and safest method of fertilization among bonsai enthusiasts is using oil-dreg fertilizers. The ingredients are mixed in proportions of 7:3 of oil-dreg and bone meal, or 5:5 of oil-dreg and fish meal, respectively. Mix them in water and knead into small balls. Put the balls in the sun to dry, and reserve them for later use. You can also mix oil-dreg with about 20% of tree and grass ashes, and add bone meal to the mixture several days later. By doing this, the potassium supply will increase and the components of the ashes will saponify the oil in the oil-dreg to enhance the effects of fertilization. When fertilizing, put the solid fertilizers on the edge of the pot soil. Daily watering will dissolve them, and they will slowly permeate the soil to be absorbed by the roots.

Timing for fertilization

The best times to fertilize trees are in spring and fall after the new buds have opened or when the trees are growing vigorously because at these times the trees are capable of absorbing more nutrition. However, do not fertilize miscellaneous varieties in spring, because this will cause the lengthening of the internodes, which affects the density and compactness of the design. An environment with temperatures between 68°F and 77°F and relative humidity between 70% and 90% is ideal for bonsai growth. The best time to fertilize the tree is after a rainfall or watering when the soil is moist, because fertilizers can more easily penetrate the soil and disperse evenly. With flowering varieties, fertilizers should be applied immediately after the flowering stage; this is called post-flowering fertilization. If a potassium fertilizer is applied to fruiting varieties after the flowering period, they will produce good crops of fruit.

Oil-dreg.

Bone meal.

Solid oil-dreg fertilizer.

Solid fertilizers applied on bonsai soil surface.

These five photos show how to mix oil-dreg and bone meal (or fish meal) to make solid fertilizer.

Methods of applying fertilizers

When oil-dreg fertilizers are applied, the dregs should be placed one inch apart from the rim of the pot soil because the roots of the bonsai first extend to the rim of the pot and then grow downward. Moreover, because the soil near the rim is drier and the pot temperature there higher, roots at the edge of the pot have greater absorbing capacity. If liquid fertilizer is used, it should be applied to the roots or the leaf surface. When the pot soil is prepared for fertilization, the level of the soil in the center should be a little higher to expose the root-base, and the soil at the rim should be slightly lower to allow better penetration of water and fertilizers.

Potted trees grow most rapidly and vigorously during the spring rains and in early summer. If the grower feeds the bonsai with liquid fertilizers, increasing the amount by 30%, the trees, especially young trees or half-established trees repotted within the previous two months, grow more vigorously. However, avoid using solid fertilizers during rainy periods because rain causes them to break down, clogging the soil pores and hindering ventilation, which may result in root decay.

Potted trees also grow vigorously in summer. Because both temperature and rate of evaporation are high, nitrogenous fertilizers should be applied more frequently. Even when using regular liquid fertilizers, be sure to add 30% more water to dilute them and water the tree prior to fertilizing. Besides placing pieces of oil-dreg on the soil surface, water the soil with a liquid fertilizer once a week to prevent loss of vigor. For trees of the pine and juniper families, use a nitrogen fertilizer with 1:1000 dilution and spray the solution on the leaves at five in the afternoon to obtain best results. Don't fertilize the plant at once after pruning. It is safer to wait one month to fertilize after repotting.

Generally, the failure of fertilization is largely due to inadequate watering, dry pot soil, or the application of concentrated liquid fertilizer. If the applied liquid fertilizer has a higher concentration than the water in the root cells, the roots not only fail to absorb the food but also lose their water content, resulting in root burn. Therefore, fertilizers must be applied frequently but sparingly; and, prior to application, the tree must be sufficiently watered to ensure an even distribution of fertilizer.

Emergency treatment for over-fertilizing

The key to fertilizing is to feed the tree frequently but sparingly. Strong fertilizers must not be used. In case a strong fertilizer is used and the roots are burnt, immerse the tree in a pail of water for two to three hours. Then remove the tree and put it in a shady and cool place. If the damage is serious, immediate pruning, transplanting and repotting are necessary.

Control of pests and diseases

Environmental pollution has become very serious in recent years. Exhaust from cars pollutes the atmosphere, while toxic wastes from factories contaminate rivers and lakes. Air and water pollution are growing worse every day and threaten the well-being of bonsai in many ways. It would be extremely distressing to discover one day that, after so much care and effort, your bonsai are ravaged by pests and diseases. It is, therefore, important to guard against pests and diseases.

Daily observation

When doing routine watering and maintenance work, observe the condition of the bonsai carefully. Examine (1) the color and shape of the leaves to see if they are in normal condition, (2) the tree's growth to see if there are any drastic or sudden changes, and (3) the tree for signs of disease or insect attack. If the trees are suffering from disease or insect infestation, the grower must, first, ascertain what kinds of insects or diseases are destroying the trees by analyzing the body structure of the insects and the degree of damage. Then, the best treatment for the trees and the means to eliminate the insects can be determined.

Causes of insect damage

Insects survive the cold season by remaining dormant. When spring comes and the temperature begins to rise, they grow and reproduce rapidly and then begin to eat the plants, causing serious damage. Usually, the destructive activities of insects reach their peak around late September. If the bonsai grower overlooks pest control, his plants will definitely suffer serious injury. Pest control is especially important during rainy periods when humidity is high. Other problems can promote insect damage: (1) incorrect application of toxic chemical compounds, underfeeding or overfeeding, and air pollution, (2) climatic elements such as low temperature, high humidity, strong winds, frosts, etc., (3) improper soil and poor drainage, which result in poor root growth, and (4) inadequate sunlight and spacing between trees.

The polluted environment of the city results in unfavorable plant growth.

Bonsai plants need lots of sunlight.

Aphids are a frequently-seen pest feeding on the sap of plants and causing damage.

Scale insects attach themselves to leaves and buds.

Pests and their control

Aphids: These sap-sucking insects may be found anywhere, in any tree species. They attack new buds, leaves, and stems, causing foliage to wilt and the health of the tree to deteriorate. They can also infect the tree with a disease called leaf wilt, which causes serious damage. As a general rule, aphids are most active in spring and fall. To eliminate aphids, spray affected trees with fenitrothion and malathion twice in one operation.

Scale insects: These pests attack more than 37 genera and 76 species of trees. They are usually found on the branches, trunk, roots, or leaf stalks. They suck tree-sap and have protective coloring. Scale insects can be eradicated by using fenitrothion, dimethoate, or lime-and-sulphur solution.

Red spiders: These are very small insects, wingless and usually red. They flock together to eat buds and leaves. Affected leaves will lose their proper color and finally fall. Red spiders are highly resistant to insecticides. For eradication, use two or three kinds of insecticides that destroy adult insects as well as eggs. Two consecutive sprayings a week will produce better results. To kill red spiders, spray affected parts with dicofol or chinomethionate.

Root-knot nematodes: Nematode disease is caused by tiny worms found in the roots underground. They can form galls or knots and cause root decay, which usually starts from the epidermal layer. For prevention, sterilize the soil with dibromochloropropane.

Lace bugs: Frequently found in Satsuki azaleas and azaleas, these sap-sucking insects thrive in hot and dry weather and live on the underside of leaves. To control them, spray the leaves with fenitrothion, malathion, or water.

Leaf rollers: These insects excrete threads that winds around leaves. When the affected leaves are uncurled, tiny green insects can be found inside. To eradicate them, press the curled leaves with the fingers to kill the insects or spray the leaves three or four times weekly with fenitrothion or dichlorvos.

Snails: Snails are mollusks. They hide in the pot or on the undersides of leaves in the daytime and come out to eat young leaves, petals, and fruits at night. The sticky substance they secrete has a silvery color when dry. Snails are usually killed with bait; granular bait is the most effective kind but its effect is not long-lasting. If the bait is mixed with some beer in a tray the results will be improved.

The most common plant pest is the caterpillar.

Insect eggs laid on the underside of a leaf.

Red spiders are among the smallest plant pests.

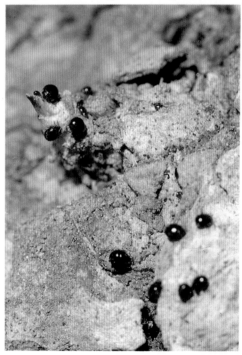

Bait   Beer

Slug Bait Killing Method

A snail hidden in the bark of a tree trunk.

A hanging basket-worm.

Plant diseases and their prevention

Powdery mildew: This disease is characterized by the presence of a whitish, powdery mildew on new buds, flower stalks, young stems, and the surface or underside of leaves. It distorts foliage and causes leaves to fall. Generally, this disease is spread on hot days and humid nights. Overapplication of nitrogen fertilizers is also a possible cause. Affected trees should be sprinkled with mancozeb or lime-and-sulphur solution.

Rust: In the initial stage of rust damage, dark purple specks may be seen on the leaf surface. These then enlarge into round or irregular spots that are at first orange and later turn brownish red. For prevention, spray the tree with mancozeb or oxycarboxin and lime-and-sulphur solution from April through October.

Red mildew: This disease is commonly found in pear and flowering quince. Reddish brown spots appear on the surface of the foliage. If the disease becomes serious, it will infect the fruit. Spray with mancozeb for effective control.

Spotted with disease: The first signs of this disease are black spots on the leaf surface. Then the affected leaves will turn completely yellow. This disease occurs in early summer when the air is moist. Therefore, pruning the branches and foliage, maintaining good air circulation, and keeping the leaf surface dry are effective methods of prevention. For treatment, spray with polyoxin once every three or four days.

White mould: This disease is common in miscellaneous and fruiting varieties. It often occurs at the end of the rainy season or in early fall. A whitish, powdery substance can be found at the tips of twigs and leaves, which subsequently fall. Spray captan on sick trees for effective treatment.

Anthracnose: This disease spots and distorts foliage. The spots first appear as concave areas that become irregular and eventually form sunken rings, which are more noticeable in succulent leaves. Anthracnose occurs most frequently in the rainy weather and in fall. To control the disease, spray affected trees with dithane or orthocide two or three times every ten days.

Leaf damage from moth larvae.

Guidelines for applying pesticides

Application of pesticides should be done on a windless morning or in the evening when the sunlight is dim or it is cloudy. Choose a time when the temperature is low and the soil is dry.

Human safety should be the foremost concern. Attention should also be paid to plant safety as well as the effect pesticides have on pest control and the environment.

Things to notice before spraying

(1) Use the correct pesticides.

(2) Use protective clothes and equipment. Do not expose the skin. Wear long-sleeved coveralls, a hat, a mask, gloves, and goggles, etc., to prevent contamination.

(3) Adjust the sprayer and sprinkler properly and make sure they work.

(4) Read the label instructions carefully and follow them strictly; pay special attention to the amount and method used to dilute the pesticide.

(5) Give advance notice to neighbors. Children, old people, and the sick should not come near.

(6) Make sure that no pesticide contaminates laundry or toys.

Things to notice while spraying

(1) Stand with your back to the wind so that the pesticide does not contaminate your body.

(2) Never smoke while applying pesticides.

(3) If the sprayer does not work, do not blow on it or touch it with your hands.

Things to observe after spraying

(1) After spraying, carefully clean all spraying equipment and empty the sprayer completely.

(2) Dig a hole in the ground and bury the residue in it.

(3) Empty pesticide bottles or packets should be stored in a safe place. Do not put them near food or beverages or places accessible to children. If they are to be reserved for another use, wash and clean them thoroughly.

(4) After spraying, wash your face, hands, and feet with plenty of soap.

(5) Keep children away from the area being sprayed.

Pesticides will have no effect if distributed unevenly. If a pesticide that is too strong is used, plant injury will occur. Powdery mildew, rust, aphids, etc., are usually found on the underside of leaves; and, if distribution is uneven, the surviving bacteria and insects will recover very quickly and cause greater damage.

Leaf damage from plant pests.

Leaf damage from boll weevil.

Symptoms of red mildew disease.

Early symptoms of spotted wilt disease.

Symptoms of rust disease.

Symptoms of root-knot disease.

Symptoms of anthracnose disease.

Safe application of pesticides

Garden pesticides

The sale and application of DDT, BHC, and other organic mercury compounds, which have been prohibited because they are highly toxic and do not decompose easily, are likely to cause serious damage to humans, animals, and the environment.

Pesticides used in domestic gardening should be mild in nature. Try to choose a pesticide that has low toxicity, short effect, and low volatility (granular pesticides are the least volatile). Insecticides such as rotenone and fungicides such as dinocap, triazine, and folpet are suitable for garden plants grown on the ground.

Plant injury

Any sudden, abnormal reaction of plants, seeds, or bulbs to the application of pesticides is considered plant injury. Examples are chlorosis, leaf spot, and the falling of leaves and fruit.

In addition, retarded growth, malformation, scorching, long internodes, and decreased rate of germination in seeds and bulbs are also considered plant injury.

It is wiser to take preventive measures than to look for possible causes after damage. Therefore, before applying a pesticide, read the directions on the label very carefully to understand where the pesticide should be applied and whether it can be mixed with other pesticides.

Causes of plant injury

(1) The type of pesticide used: Each type of pesticide has its own particular physiological effects on plants. Different pesticides will cause different reactions.

(2) The species of the plant: Different plants and species have different degrees of resistance to pesticides.

(3) The sensitivity of the plant to the pesticide during different growing stages: Seedlings and trees in bloom have weaker resistance to pesticides and may easily suffer injuries.

(4) The ecological habitat of the plant: Resistance to pesticides also varies with the living environment of the plant.

(5) Varying environmental conditions: Some pesticides can be harmful to certain plants in intense sunlight, high temperatures, or damp soil conditions.

(6) Sub-standard pesticides: Inferior or deteriorated pesticides contain many impurities and are likely to cause injuries.

(7) Improper methods of application: Over-concentrated solutions, over-dosage, frequent applications, and inappropriate time of application are common causes of plant injury. In addition, insufficient sunlight, weak growth, poor absorption of nutrition, and wounds are also possible contributors.

(8) Application of the wrong kind of pesticide: Follow the directions on the label and use the correct pesticide.

(9) Application of multiple pesticides: Applying several pesticides simultaneously is likely to cause undesirable reactions.

(10) Application of pesticides with other materials: Applying pesticides and microelements or plant hormones at the same time can also cause plant injury.

If the pesticides used are too strong, they may kill nearby goldfish or tropical fishes. All pesticides must, therefore, be handled with extreme caution. Do not dirty the labels on the bottles or packages or otherwise make the instructions difficult to read.

Pesticide control

Certain pesticides have an unstable nature; if they are not controlled or stored properly, they may lose their effectiveness or, to a greater extent, poison their surroundings. Emulsifiable concentrates and fumigants are dangerous and should be handled as inflammable material. General points to observe are:

(1) All pesticides must be protected against dampness, direct sunlight, high temperature, etc. Emulsifiable concentrates and fumigants must be stored in a place suitable for dangerous material.

(2) Prevent direct skin contact with pesticides. Wash skin with soap and water or disinfectant after every pesticide application. Before entering the pesticide storage room, open all windows. Do not enter until good ventilation is available to prevent inhalation of toxic air.

(3) The pesticide storage room must be dry and well-ventilated. Room temperature should be below 95°F and relative humidity below 80%.

(4) Be careful when pesticides are moved. If there is breakage or leakage, replace or destroy the damaged containers at once. Make sure that the caps of bottles of emulsifiable concentrates are fastened tightly.

(5) Certain pesticides decompose when heated and can release toxic fumes that are detrimental to health. Some pesticides are inflammable and care should be taken to avoid exposing them to high heat.

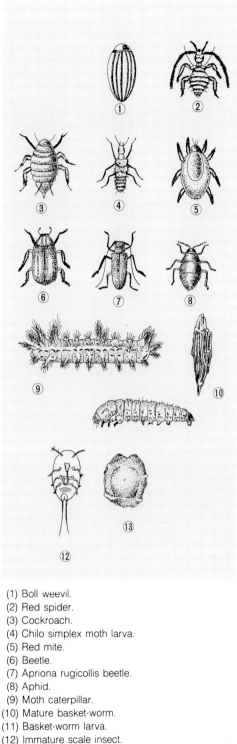

(1) Boll weevil.
(2) Red spider.
(3) Cockroach.
(4) Chilo simplex moth larva.
(5) Red mite.
(6) Beetle.
(7) Apriona rugicollis beetle.
(8) Aphid.
(9) Moth caterpillar.
(10) Mature basket-worm.
(11) Basket-worm larva.
(12) Immature scale insect.
(13) Mature scale insect.

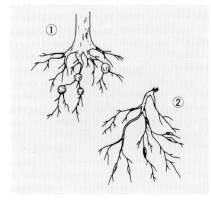

(1) Symtoms of root knots.
(2) Symptoms of nematodes.

HOW TO CHOOSE TREE
MATERIALS

A strong and beautiful root-base (Japanese red maple).

A natural bend in the top of a trunk-base (Formosan buckthorn).

A beautiful combination of a stretched root-base and handsome trunk-base (Trident maple).

How to Choose Tree Materials

Any variety of tree can be planted in a pot, but not every potted tree can become a superior bonsai. Therefore, the bonsai enthusiast must be very cautious in selecting good tree materials in order to cultivate and create an excellent bonsai. If inferior materials are chosen, it takes twice the effort to create a bonsai. When a bonsai is half-finished, it is also difficult to remedy defects. The necessary qualities of ideal bonsai materials are as follows:

Choose a tree with a good root-base and many fine roots

Roots anchor the tree in the pot. The part of the root system that is exposed on the soil surface is called the root-base. Choose a root-base with strong, vigorous, and shallow surface roots that radiate outward evenly, because such a root-base best displays stability. Moreover, only shallow and even roots can grow in a shallow pot when the tree is finally made into a bonsai. The root-base of a tree is the symbol of a bonsai's age. After a long time, the surface roots spread out in the shape of a chicken's claw and greatly enhance the beauty of the bonsai. Choosing a good root-base is very important because the technique of creating roots is extremely difficult. The quality of the root-base can be judged clearly by examining the roots while they are exposed to the air. In addition, the suitable tree should have many fine roots so that the bonsai grows more easily. The best root-base is one with stretched roots.

Choose a tree material that has a handsome trunk-base, natural beauty, and variety

The part of the trunk between the root-base and the first branch is called the trunk-base. Generally, it should be in the shape of a trumpet, which is wide at the bottom and narrow at the top. The ideal position of the first branch should be at one third of the height of the tree, on a scale of 1:1.5 or 1:2, which is ideal for shaping and training purposes. A shaped tree that is based on this scale best displays harmony and stability; it is considered the golden scale in bonsai creation.

The choice of a bonsai style is dependent upon the pattern of the trunk-base. For instance, if the trunk-base is straight, the tree may be grown into an upright style; if the trunk-base is curved and angular, it may be shaped into a slanting, coiled, or twisted-trunk style; if the trunk-base is short, the trunk small, and branches low, it may be made into a miniature bonsai. A tree with a tall trunk-base, a thick trunk, and high branches may be cultivated into a medium or large bonsai. Because the trunk-base is not concealed by branches or foliage, it is essential to choose one without wounds or scars, or the beauty of the bonsai will be diminished. Choosing tree material that has a good root-base and a fine trunk-base with pattern and variety means that the bonsai enthusiast is already halfway to success in the process of creation. The importance of the choice of a good trunk-base is unquestionable.

Choose tree materials with aged bark and scarless trunks that taper evenly from the base to the apex

The trunk is the skeleton of a bonsai; the most ideal material is a round and scarless single trunk. Generally, tree material with a round trunk has a better root-base. If there are cuts on the trunk, the possibility of healing them should be taken into consideration, especially in a deciduous variety. Otherwise, the side with the cuts should not be put in front. The wounds have direct influence on the number of years a bonsai can live. If the wounds cannot be healed, they will spread widely to cause withered branches or trunks and damage the layout. A good trunk must taper from a thick base to a delicate apex, but if it lacks a taper and is narrow at the base, even though the root-base may be well formed, the tree will appear top-heavy and seem on the verge of falling. The trunk may also be erect or have curves and irregular patterns according to the characteristics of each tree species and the chosen manner of expression. Chapped or wrinkled bark best exhibits the appearance of aged trees in bonsai. The thickness of the trunk and the height of the tree must be in harmony with the overall tree shape.

A plant which has a completely natural shari appearance (Japanese premna).

A plant with an elegant root-base and branches (Formosan hackberry).

A flowing trunk without a trace of scarring (Trident maple).

A plant with a profusion of tiny leaves (Reef pemphis).

A plant with dense and well-shaped growth of branches (Japanese gray-bark elm).

A plant with a dense profusion of branches that are emphasized by changes in season (Japanese gray-bark elm)

Choose tree materials with branches at ideal positions

For a better three-dimensional effect, choose a tree with branches shooting from favorable positions and growing upward in a clockwise or counter-clockwise direction. It is better to choose a tree with steady growth patterns so that its branches will not elongate or thicken abruptly. The tree should also be able to produce branchlets and auxiliary buds readily. In addition, the tree should be thornless and have fine twigs and short internodes. A tree with thick branches on its lower portion and finer branches toward the top best imparts the illusion of a massive tree. (However, a sense of wildness can add to the overall effect if there are some comparatively thicker and longer branches at the top.) Deciduous varieties, in particular, have dense branches and best display a sense of massiveness. If the tree has whorled branches (i.e. many branches extending from the same point) and some of the thick branches are removed, unsightly bulges will often form at the severing point, particularly in the black pine. Only when the branches are still thin, therefore, can the bonsai cultivator selectively retain those that grow out at favorable positions.

Choose tree materials with good foliage

Leaves can be likened to the coat of the tree. They are also the focal point for the viewer. A tree must have dense, small, flat, simple leaves in order to be made into a medium or small bonsai or even a miniature bonsai. Conversely, a tree with broad opposing leaves can only be cultivated into a large or medium bonsai. Choose a tree with succulent, well-shaped, and even leaves because they show the firmness, order, and liveliness of the overall shape of the bonsai. The color of the buds should be red or white. If the tree is an evergreen variety, choose one with lustrous green leaves; if it is a deciduous variety, choose one whose leaves show seasonal color changes clearly because this will enhance the value of the tree.

Choose tree materials with heavy crops of fruit as well as fragrant and beautiful flowers

Flowers should be of bright color and full of variety. A tree that can produce flowers of more than two different colors is an excellent choice. The size of the flowers must be in proportion to the tree. Flowers that are too large should be avoided. The ideal flowering tree material should have pleasant fragrance, thick petals, a long flowering period, and flowers that bloom at the same time. In choosing a fruiting tree, make sure that its pollination and fertilization are easy and that the color of the fruit is pleasing and in contrast to the color of the leaves. Choose a tree that has a long flowering and fruiting period and whose flowers and fruit do not fall easily. Generally speaking, shrubs bloom more easily than trees and, in the case of dioecious plants, the female plants bloom more easily than the male.

Choose tree materials without insect damage that are available at reasonable price

A tree infected by pests is weak and will most likely die. If it survives, it will lack vigor and need fertilizer for a long period of time in order to recover. Care and maintenance of the tree are also difficult. The insects may infect other healthy bonsai and cause irreparable damage such as withered branches or stems that affects the beauty of the bonsai.

When purchasing tree materials, the bonsai enthusiast should choose quality rather than quantity; owning too many bonsai may impede proper care. Bonsai lovers, especially beginners, should avoid the temptation to buy a great quantity of cheap and poor materials. Do not blindly follow fashion without regard for personal taste. A suitable plan that matches one's own abilities and level of bonsai appreciation must be developed and tree materials bought to correspond with this plan.

A favorably sprouting plant (Black pine).

A beautifully leafy plant (Chinese hackberry).

Colorful and beautifully shaped blossoms (Satsuki azalea).

PROPAGATION OF BONSAI STOCK

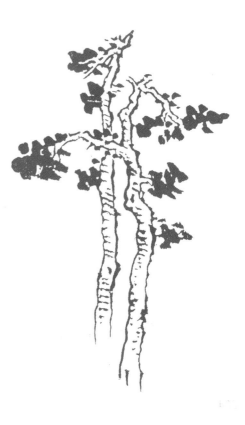

Planting Sargent juniper from the mountains.

Cultivating fragrant maple from the mountains.

A Taiwan fire-thorn tree taken from the wilds planted in a bonsai container.

Propagation of Bonsai Stock

Bonsai stock is the source of bonsai material. It is chiefly obtained by (A) collecting from the mountains, (B) sowing, (C) cutting, (D) layering, (E) grafting, or (F) separating or dividing. The bonsai lover can derive a great deal of enjoyment from growing his own trees from bonsai stock.

All of the methods for obtaining bonsai stock make use of plants' nutritional organs and the recycling functions of plant tissue or certain plant parts to produce new plants similar to mother plants. This process is called asexual reproduction.

Collecting from the mountains

The avid bonsai hunter scours through mountains to dig up suitable tree materials for use as bonsai stock. This method of collecting tree materials was once used to obtain old, prized trees. The current worldwide movement to promote ecological balance and conservation of resources, however, makes this pursuit questionable.

When collecting trees, choose those that grow in shallow, poor sandy areas or sunny places. A tree material that has aged bark, well-formed surface roots, a short trunk, dense branches, and small and thick foliage can be trained and grown into a handsome bonsai within a short period of time. Don't lose yourself in the pleasure of nature and forget the above-mentioned principles while collecting bonsai stock. How can old, bulky trunks with wounds and bad root-bases be transformed into handsome bonsai? Because old trees have not been transplanted for many years, they have many thick roots; moreover, they may be weakened by living in a harsh environment. The season and method of collection should be carefully considered; otherwise, the tree materials may be useless.

Collecting season

For trees in the frigid and temperate zones, the best collecting season is spring, before new buds open. After winter dormancy, with the gradual rise in temperature, the tree buds are ready to open, and, because cell division is very rapid and roots grow easily, the chance of survival is greater.

Tropical varieties such as common jasmin orange, banyan, Chinese hackberry, Chinese podocarpus, and reef pemphis cannot be collected until April when the difference in temperature between day and night will be less, stabilizing at around 77°F. Fall is also a suitable collecting season. In Taiwan, however, typhoon season comes in July and August and the temperature is high. It is, therefore, better to wait until late September or October to collect bonsai stock.

Because climate varies every year and tree species and temperatures also vary from one place to another, study the growing conditions of individual species to discover suitable times for collection.

Procedures for collection in the mountains

Prepare the tools: These include hoes, small shovels, saws, scissors, a water tank, sphagnum moss, small ropes, polythene paper bags, and straw ropes. They should be ready before going to the mountains.

Select the front-facing side: When suitable tree material has been found, examine its four sides carefully and determine which is to be the front. Then saw off the unwanted portion of the trunk and any abnormally long branches. Seal the wound immediately with a tree sealant to prevent both the attack of disease microorganisms and dehydration, which can cause branches to wither. Because conifers do not send out roots easily, it is necessary to retain more leaves on the branches when they are trimmed. The leaf surface can directly absorb the moisture and nutrients necessary to maintain the minimal life mechanism of the tree.

Clean the root-base: Use tools to carefully remove the soil and grass around the surface roots. If there are many thick roots, cut them at suitable positions. Roots on the sides can be long, but those in front and back should be cut short. It is better to cut off those roots that point downward and retain the fine roots that radiate from the root-base so that the tree can be planted in a shallow container. Wounds should then be covered with sphagnum moss and earth. Use a tripod to prop up the trunk and fix the tree firmly. After two or three months of watering, the tree will send out fine roots, and it will be time to dig it up. Some bonsai enthusiasts have suggested recently that the tree be dug at once upon discovery; they suggest that by doing so the tree is left stronger and better able to survive.

Dig carefully: When a conifer is being dug, it is essential to retain the surrounding earth. The size of the soil-ball should be four times the diameter of the trunk-base. The extension of roots from right to left depends on the condition of the root-base and the bonsai style the grower intends to create. The roots have to be cut with a sharp knife so that the wounds are even and new roots can grow easily. When digging a tree, dig outward from the base of the tree to avoid breaking the soil-ball.

Immediate treatment: After the tree is dug, tie the roots and soil-ball with straw ropes to prevent the soil-ball from breaking. Next, cover the roots with wet sphagnum moss and tie them up in a plastic bag. Roots without a soil-ball are also treated in the same way. In addition, spray the trunk and foliage with water and transport the tree to the nursery quickly. Do not linger at the spot trying to find more tree materials because the tree may die of dehydration.

Moral obligation: Places such as preservation areas, national parks, and government-owned forests strictly prohibit collecting. In other places, the collector must first obtain permission before digging; and, when the digging is done, he must fill the hollow and level the ground. When collecting tree materials, the bonsai enthusiast should look for quality rather than quantity. Do not dig too many trees at one time or ecological balance will be disrupted.

How to grow tree materials collected from the mountains

After the collected tree has been transported home, water the trunk and foliage first. Unwrap the package and remove unwanted

Fukien tea collected from the mountains.

Planted in a cultivating container to maintain moisture.

New shoots begin to sprout.

The same plant two years later.

Selected seeds soaking in a beaker.

Segregated germination of seeds.

Scattered germination of seeds.

The application of fertilizer to seedling transplants.

branches. Use a sharp knife to cut evenly. Dress the wounds with a tree sealant to help them heal. Cut downward-growing and unnecessary bulky roots where tiny roots grow out. The cuts must be trimmed evenly so that a handsome root-base can be formed. Thus, when the tree is made into a bonsai, it may be planted in a shallow pot. Use a sharp knife to cut radial roots and make sure that the cuts are even and face downward. Choose well-drained granular soil mixed correctly for the characteristics of the tree being trained. Areas around the severed roots must be covered first with sphagnum moss and then with fine granular soil. (New roots can grow easily 2 in. to 4 in. below the soil surface.) Fix the tree firmly to prevent it from moving so that newly grown fine roots will not be damaged or wilt. Put the transplanted tree in a shady, damp place and water the leaves frequently. Because the tree has lost most of its vigor and the absorbing capacity of its roots after being transplanted, it should be put in a place with a mild temperature and high humidity.

For coniferous varieties, water the leaves frequently and sufficiently. Sprinkle with diluted root catalyst to induce root growth. For deciduous tree material, such as Chinese elm, Japanese gray-bark elm (zelkova), trident maple, and Japanese maple, use a transparent polythene bag to wrap the tree tightly. This helps to maintain the moisture in the trunk and branches, and the temperature inside the bag rises and accelerates the opening of new buds. After the second budding, cut the polythene bag from the bottom to the top. Allow the new buds to adjust to their new growing environment before removing the bag. It is better to grow tree materials collected from the mountains temporarily on the ground or in large unglazed pots; this is extremely helpful in restoring the vigor of trees, healing the cuts, and improving defects.

Sowing

This is a technique of cultivating bonsai materials by sowing seeds to germinate into seedlings, which are called new or young trees. By this method, the bonsai grower can create bonsai styles according to his own preferences, and the tree materials also maintain their particular characteristics perfectly. This sowing method accords well with current trends toward ecological protection and will become the mainstay of bonsai propagation in future. Some advantages of sowing are as follows: a large amount of bonsai stock can be propagated from the ripe seeds of superior species collected in the fall. Using his imagination or imitating prize bonsai, the grower can train his stock into desirable shapes. Moreover, trees grown from seeds usually have better potential for becoming superior bonsai. For bonsai enthusiasts who pursue perfection in the art of bonsai, this is the best method to use. Seeds collected in the fall, with the exception of fruit species that require immediate sowing, should usually be sown between February and April when the potential for germination is greatest.

Procedures for sowing

Collect seeds: Choose the seeds from trees with superior qualities for developing into bonsai. Collect seeds after they are ripe. Dry and store them in a tightly sealed bottle or bag. Then hang the container in a dry area with good ventilation, or put it in a polythene bag and bury it under the ground.

Methods of planting cuttings:
(1) Slanted insertion (insert ½ or ⅓ into the soil).
(2) Soil ball insertion (insert ½ or ⅓ into the soil).
(3) Perpendicular insertion (insert ½ or ⅓ into the soil).

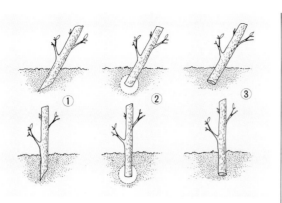

Group cultivation of black pine seedlings.

Select seeds: Store seeds in the refrigerator one week to one month before sowing. Soak seeds in water the night before sowing. Those that sink to the bottom are good, fully ripe seeds that are sure to germinate. Discard those that float to the surface of the water.

Prepare the seed bed: Prepare a suitable seed bed. This can be either an unglazed pot or a wooden box with a height of 4 in. to 6 in. and good drainage. First of all, place a plastic net over the bottom holes. Cover this with one or two layers of coarse sand (0.2 in. to 0.3 in.) and fill the container with fine soil (0.04 in. to 0.1 in.).

Methods of sowing: Sprinkle small seeds over the soil. Plant larger seeds in strips in the earth or bury them one by one in holes dug with the fingers. Plant the top of the seed downward to produce a good root-base. After the seeds are sown, cover them with soil to a depth twice their diameter. Big seeds must be covered by much more soil. After sowing, water the soil.

Control after sowing: After sowing, place the seed bed in a place with partial shade and good ventilation. Water it carefully, and do not allow it to be covered by dust or allow the seeds to be exposed to the air. Spray the seed bed with water to prevent it from drying up. After about 30 to 40 days, when the first pair of leaves opens, move the seedlings to a position where they receive direct sunlight. Use the fingers to draw ditches around the seedling and apply oil dregs as fertilizers to promote growth.

Cutting

Short pieces of roots, branches, or leaves can be cut from varieties of trees that send out adventitious roots and buds easily; these cuttings should then be planted in pots or wooden boxes. The difference between cutting and layering to propagate plants is that, in cutting, the cut parts produce new parts after being separated from the mother tree.

Cutting is a very simple and easy technique for propagation. Even beginners learn it easily. With this method, it is easy to obtain propagated materials bearing the same characteristics as the parent tree. Cuttings taken from flowering and fruiting varieties develop flowers and fruits in a short time, much faster than a seedling grown from seeds. Thus cutting has become a widely applied method of propagating bonsai stock. Bonsai stock grown by cutting is called new stock.

Inserting Sargent juniper cuttings for group cultivation.

Methods of planting root cuttings (Chinese elm):
(1) When transplanting, arrange the roots neatly.
(2) Cut off the longer coarse roots.
(3) Trim the roots to an appropriate length.
(4) Pour a bed of coarse soil in a container.
(5) Cover the coarse soil with fine soil.
(6) Insert the prepared roots into the cutting bed.
(7) A view of newly sprouted root growth.
(8) A cutting propagated using the root insertion method.

Seasons for planting cuttings

Generally, there are three suitable seasons for planting cuttings: spring, before the new buds open; the rainy season in early summer when young shoots are turgid and becoming woody; and fall.

Procedures in planting cuttings

Take care of the parent tree before taking cuttings: Before taking cuttings, the parent tree should be given extra fertilizers and pesticides so that cuttings taken from it have a better chance to survive and grow. Use apical or strong, long branches for cuttings because they survive best.

Prepare cuttings: When taking cuttings, use a sharp knife or scissors. The ideal length of the cutting is about 1 in. to 2 in. of dominant shoots or 4 in. of the roots. The cutting may be straight, slanted, opposite, split, or Split-slanted (see illustration). Soak the lower end of the cutting in a dilute solution of root catalyst for 20 – 30 minutes to absorb sufficient moisture. Then use a sharp knife to trim the cuts so that a smooth root-base can be formed. Retain only two or three leaves on the branches and prune the rest.

Prepare the cutting bed: Cuttings may be planted in an unglazed pot or a wooden box 4 in. to 6 in. high. First, cover the bottom drainage holes with plastic screening. Then spread a layer of coarse soil on top and fill the container with a soil mixture of clay and sand in a ratio of 8:2.

Plant cuttings: Cuttings should be planted in such a way that their leaves touch but do not overlap. One-third to half of the length of the cuttings should be buried in the soil. They may either be planted slantingly (to produce coiled and slanting styles) or upright (for upright styles), with the cuts facing downward due to the geotropic nature of roots. Another way to plant cuttings is to mix earth with water and make a small soil ball. Plant shoots in the soil balls. Make the cuttings and the balls as tight as possible.

Control after cutting

After planting, water the cuttings sufficiently with the dilute root catalyst previously used to soak them. All cuttings should be protected from direct sunlight and strong winds. It is desirable to grow them in a nursery. Spray the cuttings two or three times a day and start fertilizing them with oil dregs in ditches around the seedlings after six months.

A grafting cut of 1 in. to 2 in. is ideal.

The lower portion of a cutting trimmed to produce two angled surfaces.

Fertilized inserted cuttings.

Cutting methods:

Split-slanted cut.   Split cut.   Opposite cut.   Slanted cut.   Straight cut.

Metal wire-winding layering method.

Tongue-cutting layering method.

Wave-cutting layering method.

Ring-cutting layering method.

Layering

In this method, trees that easily send out adventitious roots and buds are used to improve the growth of long internodes, long or heavy apical branches, or ugly root-bases to achieve balance and harmony in the design of the tree. This method of encouraging new roots to grow at desirable positions and separating new trees from the parent tree is called layering.

There are three kinds of layering: bend layering, mound layering, and height layering. The methods of cutting to acquire stock are ring-cutting, wave-cutting, tongue-cutting, crescent-cutting, and metal wire-winding.

The application of height layering

For deciduous trees, layering is usually done in April and May when the new leaves begin to mature; for evergreens, it is done from late April to July. First of all, decide upon the plant part to be layered. If height layering is used, ring-bark the section below the point where roots are expected to grow. Remove the bark, the cambium, and part of the xylem to reduce the sieve vessels' ability to transport water and nutrition and increase the healing ability of the tree. The carbohydrate absorbed by sieve vessels can accelerate the growth of roots. The length of the cut should be approximately twice the diameter of the trunk or branch on which the layer is taken. If the ring-barked section is not wide enough, the bark may heal over and fail to send out roots. Use a sharp knife to smooth out the upper line of the cut and allow it to dry. Apply insecticide and then cover the section with sphagnum moss or red clay pre-soaked in a dilute solution of root catalyst. Wrap the area with a polythene sheet. Make a cut in the top of the plastic sheet to facilitate watering and punch several holes in the bottom for drainage. Before roots begin to appear, water the layer several times a day to keep the sphagnum moss moist but make sure that it is not too damp or too dry so that the layer can send out roots. Sever the layer from the parent tree when the new roots become mature and brown in color; then remove the plastic sheet but retain the sphagnum moss. Plant the layer in a pot and use a rope or wire to fix it in place.

Using the layering method to obtain a plant for miniature bonsai.

After the layering procedure, a beautiful and small creation is obtained.

With layering, a single garden tree can produce many types of bonsai with different appearances.

Height Layering Procedures (Japanese maple):
(1) Select an appropriate object branch.
(2) Remove the bark from around an entire section.
(3) Cover with sphagnum moss and bind with plastic sheeting.
(4) Cut the branch off when the roots are visible.
(5) The height-layering method allows the planting of a miniature bonsai.

Inarching Grafting Procedures (Japanese grey-bark elm):
(1) Make a small incision into the xylem of the stock.
(2) Remove the part of the bark around a section of the scion.
(3) Insert the scion into the stock.
(4) Fasten the scion securely. (A successful example is at lower left.)

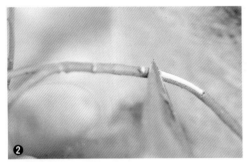

Grafting

Scions taken from superior or precious bonsai can be grafted to stocks of the same species or genera. With this method of propagation, the favorable characteristics of the parent tree can be reproduced in the new tree.

There are four methods of grafting: branch grafting, bud grafting, trunk grafting, and root grafting. Grafting requires expert skill and is not easily learned by beginners. It is now widely applied to miscellaneous bonsai species. If the bonsai lacks branches or roots in appropriate positions, new ones can be grafted on. Grafting is, therefore, a time-saving technique used to create a more perfect shape. Grafting is also used to improve inflorescence. Some varieties, such as Japanese red maple, are propagated by grafting because the grafted trees survive better and grow faster than the parent trees. (Japanese red maple does not root easily when propagated by layering or cutting.)

Methods of grafting

Branch grafting: There are various types of grafts used to prepare stock, such as saddle, splice, cleft, box, bark, tongue, and side grafts.

Bud grafting: The methods are T-budding, key-shaped grafting, cross-shaped budding, ring-grafting, and inlaying. Both bud grafting and branch grafting should be done in cool weather for a greater chance of success.

(1) Top grafting method.
(2) Side grafting method.

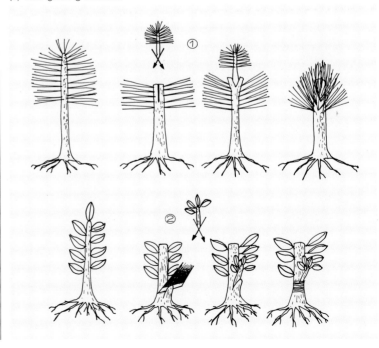

(1) Cut an appropriate branch.

Branch Grafting Procedures:
(Banyan)

(2) Cut off all branchlets except for two branch buds.

(3) Slant cut the bottom of the scion to form a sharp angled tip.

(4) Slice an angled incision into the xylem of the trunk.

Using an electric drill to bore a hole in the trunk is another way to apply grafting techniques.

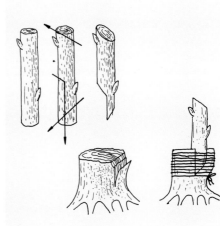

(5) Insert the scion into the trunk.

Cleft grafting method.

(6) Tightly bind the lip of the incision over the scion.

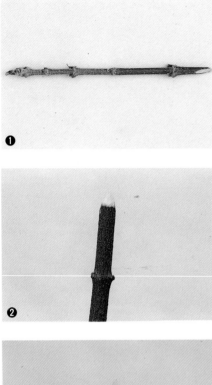

Branch Grafting Methods (Trident maple):
(1) Select a newly sprouted scion not more than a year old.
(2) Whittle the end of the trunk into a conical point.
(3) Notch the trunk at the point where the scion will contact it.
(4) Insert the scion into the trunk.

(1) Select a site along the trunk with new bud growth.

(3) Make a T-shaped incision.

(2) Cut and remove the small bud section.

(4) Insert the leaf bud section into the trunk and bind firmly.

The root grafting method is best done at an unsightly portion of the root-base.

Trunk grafting: Trunks or branches can be grafted together; this is also known as parasitical grafting. Like bud grafting, it is a widely applied method. It can be used to create branches at positions where branches are lacking or to improve inflorescence.

Root grafting: Using this method, several roots can be grafted together. If a tree's root-base extends in only one direction or is not well-formed, roots from other trees can be grafted to improve the shape of the root-base. What people commonly call root-grafting-layering is actually a combination of the methods of root grafting and layering.

Principles of grafting

Regular grafting is carried out between February and March, when the tree wakes up from winter dormancy but the buds have not opened. The stock is derived from a seedling two or three years old and is cut at about 2 in. of its height. The scion should be obtained from a branch or stem as vigorous and healthy as the stock and preferably with the same length. The key to successful grafting is to have the cambium layers of the stock and scion in perfect union. They should be bound tightly with plastic rope so that no water can penetrate. A better result can be achieved if the cuts are treated with a grafting compound to prevent water from entering and the stock and scion from dehydrating. Water the tree with a can or stand it in a pail of water. No trimming is necessary in the first year. Allow the tree to grow freely and the edges of the scion and the stock to unite perfectly. Begin trimming in the second year and use a sharp knife to smooth the cuts so that they heal well.

Separation or division

Certain plants send out suckers from the roots or the base of stems, and these suckers can grow into healthy plants when separated. Separation or division is a method of propagating bonsai stock by severing these suckers from the parent plants. Fukien tea and Japanese quince are usually propagated by this method.

Since the suckers or shoots are removed with their own roots, their chance of survival is great. When separating shoots from the parent plant, use a sharp knife and seal the cuts with a tree sealant to prevent the attack of harmful bacteria. The optimum season for separation is the transplanting season of each species.

Root Grafting Methods (Trident maple):
(1) Remove the bark around a section of the trunk.
(2) Use a sharp blade to cut a flap of bark above the stripped section.
(3) Select root cuttings from a tree of the same species.
(4) Secure the root cuttings after insertion under the bark flap and wrap with sphagnum moss.

BONSAI CREATION

Trees in their natural setting are models for the creation of bonsai.

Bonsai Creation

The artist's objective in bonsai creation is to use keen observations of nature to present the beauty of tree materials and closely reproduce natural trees in miniature. Bonsai are created through the artist's creative manipulation of tree materials. His techniques include training, shaping, and sculpting; choice of style and frontal orientation are also important. All must ensure stable growth.

Understand the shape of bonsai

Bonsai are living organisms. Two plants may have different shapes even though they are grown from the same kind of seed and given the same care. The subjective techniques of the artist also determine the shape or style of the tree. There is a great variety of shapes and forms of bonsai, each with its own special features. Although there is no consistent tree shape, there are still some guidelines to follow.

When styling a bonsai, the artist must, first of all, understand the characteristics of each tree species. Using these, the artist tries to highlight the beautiful features of the tree material and reduce its defects to create a fine work of art. Therefore, a bonsai truly represents the fusion of nature and human wisdom; it is an art that at once pursues the spirits of both nature and beauty.

A natural tree is one that grows in a natural environment and is not subjected to the manipulation of man. The form and color of its roots, trunk, and branches plus the conditions of weather and its natural setting convey beauty of line, form, movement, mood, color, and rhythm; this is what bonsai enthusiasts call the beauty of natural trees.

Cultivate aesthetic sensibility

To learn shaping techniques effectively, study nature frequently. Examine the shape and form of natural trees and use these observations as the basis for shaping bonsai. Study other bonsai specimens to learn from the artistry and techniques of other artists. Compare your observations with your own bonsai; this can be helpful in improving your techniques and cultivating a keen sensitivity to beauty. Trees in nature are viewed at a distance, but bonsai specimens may be closely studied and appreciated.

Carefully observe and study fine works to understand the secrets of shaping a beautiful bonsai; at the same time, learn to understand the difference between unreasonable shaping and natural shaping. Through accumulated experience, observation, and imitation, you will learn to produce fine works of bonsai.

Examining trees in nature gives rise to many ideas for the art of bonsai.

Simplify the design to introduce the beauty of space

A bonsai is the miniaturization of a tree in nature. Because it is miniaturized, the tree's aesthetic qualities become concentrated. The delicate arrangement of space can be used to enliven the design. This is an extremely important technique in bonsai creation. The luxuriant growth of foliage and branches in some bonsai often conceals the shape of the trunk and the important branches and leaves no space at all. This kind of bonsai does not stimulate the viewer's imagination and thus fails to impart a sense of beauty.

Plan the shape of your bonsai

There are many limitations in the creation of bonsai. Because the materials are living things, the greater the grower's creative desire, the greater the difficulties he will encounter. Try to understand the condition of the bonsai, its characteristics, its growth patterns, the flexibility of its branches, and the relationship between shaping and season. Draft a yearly schedule to care for bonsai and follow the schedule accordingly. Furthermore, shaping should be done according to the tree's physiological condition. Observe and study the tree; constantly work to produce a lively and graceful work.

Adjust the tree style through timely control

One characteristic of the art of bonsai is that a small tree can produce the illusion of a massive tree growing in nature. The purpose of shaping is to create a tree that can impart a strong or soft feeling so that there is immediate empathy between the viewer and the tree.

Suppressing apical growth so that the trunk and branches near the root-system thicken is the major concern of shaping. It is very hard to make branches thicken after trimming; similarly, it is not easy to prune or bend branches when they are thick and large. Therefore, it is better to take advantage of the opportune time to train or shape trees. Trimming and pinching (bud nipping) of apical branches should be done regularly to ensure that all branches receive equal amounts of sunlight and that branches near the roots thicken while those near the apex become finer. Bonsai maintained in this manner become exquisite and shapely.

Shaping Procedures (Sargent juniper):
(1) Determining the style of the tree.
(2) Determining the frontal orientation.
(3) Trimming the tree.
(4) Pruning the unwanted branches.

Careful design

The key to creating a fine bonsai is to study the tree material carefully to understand its characteristics and develop its innate strengths and correct or conceal its defects. Do not be impatient when shaping a tree. It is important to study the tree closely and to have a rough plan in mind before working on it. Bonsai is a landscaping art using trees as the subject. There seems to be some half-hidden intangible beauty behind each tree that fosters profound feelings. After fully understanding the form of the tree, design an appropriate shape for it, and, thereafter, use the design as the guideline for shaping.

Determining the frontal orientation and style of the tree

The bonsai designer is halfway to success if he can establish the front of bonsai correctly before creation. This must be determined by the curve of the roots and the shape of the trunk. If the wrong angle is chosen for the front, the tree can never become a superior bonsai, despite superb shaping techniques. Study the tree material on a revolving stand; it is most important to look at the tree from all sides to discern the style most suitable to the tree's

(5) Using wire bracing to adjust the projection of the branches.
(6) Creating a "jinn."
(7) Completing shaping.
(8) Transforming the tree into a superb medium-size bonsai.

natural form. Look for the following qualities: the side with the widest surface roots; the angle that displays the graceful flow of the trunk line and its variations to best advantage as well as conceals cuts or scars; the direction of the twist or curve of the lower trunk; and the side where the apex leans slightly forward. Then examine the overall form of the roots, trunk, and branches to select the most suitable side for the front and decide whether it matches the shape of the tree. Then study other parts carefully and look at the tree from different angles; try to conceal the defects and exhibit the strengths of the tree.

Exaggeration, space, and simplicity

A bonsai grows within the narrow confines of the container, and its beauty is displayed through exaggeration as well as emphasis. Exaggerating the natural tendencies of the bonsai helps transmit the artist's message to the viewer, evoking empathic feelings from the viewer and drawing the viewer's attention to a single point. Remove superfluous branches to simplify a complicated design and create space; highlight the focus of attention; harmonize and unify the separate elements to display the beauty of the overall design. Creating a bonsai that conveys the spirit of nature is the most demanding aim in bonsai creation.

Flowing branches highlighted by interspersed spacing intervals make a beautiful tree shape (Nippon hawthorn).

(1) Before pruning, the chaotic growth leaves no space between the branches and leaves (Common jasmin orange).
(2) After pruning, the spacing imparts an elegant feeling (Common jasmin orange).

TRAINING AND DWARFING
OF BONSAI

Trees in nature must be shaped and dwarfed before they can become bonsai.

Long shooting branches detract from the beauty of bonsai.

Training and Dwarfing of Bonsai

Although a potted plant's growth is restricted by the limited amount of soil available in the pot, an established bonsai still requires physiological dwarfing through pinching, through leaf trimming to retain its size and handsome shape. To dwarf the tree physiologically, it should be planted in a shallow container to suppress the growth of roots; in addition, it should be placed on a shelf where it will receive sufficient sunlight but insufficient water and fertilizer. This will stunt the growth of the roots.

If growth is restricted for a long period of time, the tree will lose vigor and become weak. Therefore, once the tree is styled into an ideal shape, it is necessary to retrain the bonsai so as to check the expansion of the tree, retain its size, inhibit the development of buds, change the direction of growth, shorten internodes, and encourage the formation of more fine branchlets. In order to prevent vigorous apical growth, pinching and leaf trimming should start first with the branches near the stock and, after a few days, with branches higher up. Another alternative is to start with weak branches or branches you want to develop. In this way, nutrition will first be allocated to lower branches, weak branches, or branches you want to develop, and apical growth, which can cause branches to weaken or wither, may be prevented.

The purpose of training

The purpose of training is to dwarf a tree by trimming, pruning, and pinching.

The terminal buds at the tip of the trunk and branches may grow constantly and suppress the development of axillary buds. If the growth of terminal buds is hindered or stopped, axillary buds can develop freely. Training is a technique that takes advantage of the self-recuperative capacity of plants. Terminal buds are pinched to encourage the growth of axillary buds so as to produce more fine branchlets. After pinching, the tree will undergo physical dwarfing and become stunted. Axillary branching makes the distribution of nutrition more even, which results in the restriction of tree growth. In addition, equal amounts of sunlight, good ventilation, and balanced growth will help prevent the growth of spindling branches and achieve physiological dwarfing. Through these techniques, the density of branches can be increased and the bonsai be developed to convey the illusion of massiveness.

Bud pinching encourages the growth of axillary buds and shortens the internodes.

By using the axillary buds, the position of the branch can be modified.

The short leaf method can improve the quality of bonsai.

The short leaf method can improve the quality of bonsai.

Training and wiring

Training includes pruning, trimming, cutting, and pinching. Wiring is used to correct the defects of trees. The principle of training is based on the way natural trees send out new shoots after some parts are broken. Wiring is utilized to imitate the natural curves of trees in nature.

Bud pinching

Plants produce smaller leaves than normal if new buds are pinched once. The technique of bud pinching can thus be utilized to reduce the size of leaves.

The number of branches in a bonsai increases with each bud pinching. The production of branches will decrease if no bud pinching is done. After pinching, the nutrition which would have gathered in the top buds will spread to every branch, producing more branches.

A general rule is to pinch buds less frequently on those parts that need to be extended and become stronger. For the bonsai that needs more branches or cannot have too many long branches, bud pinching must be done more often.

Don't pinch buds on repotted or weak trees. If bud pinching is performed on weak trees, axillary buds and side buds will not grow out readily; on the contrary, the layout of the tree will be damaged and the tree become weak. Bud pinching has to be done earlier on strong branches than on weak branches (usually 2 weeks to one month earlier) to allow the early growth of second buds. This will make the shape of the bonsai more balanced.

Training and wiring are means of simulating natural tree shapes.

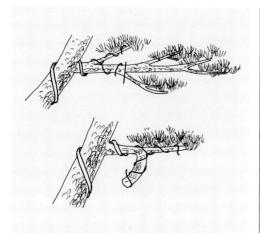

A long branch can be pruned to change its growth position.

After pruning, the method for changing the growth angle may be utilized.

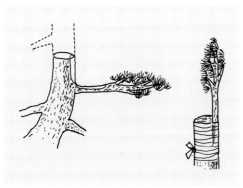

Cutting the trunk of a tall tree is a way to alter the growth pattern of the tree.

Types of buds, properties, and terminology

Buds growing at the apex of branches are called terminal buds; buds that are found at the base of branches are called lateral buds, or axillary buds. Buds growing at fixed positions are called definite buds, while those arising at places other than leaf axils are called adventitious buds. In general, pines and junipers send out definite buds, while broad-leafed varieties, like banyans, Chinese elms, and Japanese gray-bark elms, develop adventitious buds easily. Trees such as pines, maples, and Japanese gray-bark elms, which characteristically show apical dominance, exhibit vigorous bud development and expansion at the top of the tree. But certain shrubs, like azaleas, Satsuki azaleas, Taiwan fire-thorns, and flowering quinces show vigorous growth toward the bottom of the tree.

Proper methods of pinching

Leaves growing at the tip of terminal buds, lateral buds, or axillary buds produce a plant hormone called auxin. As auxin moves in the direction of the base of the shoots or leaves, it will accelerate stem growth; on the other hand, it may inhibit the growth of lateral or axillary buds. Therefore, it is necessary to pinch the terminal buds in early spring before new shoots appear. Because the first pair of leaves has not yet opened, auxin is not present to prevent the development of axillary buds.

Almost all creatures have the capacity to heal themselves when part of their body is removed. In bonsai cultivation, pinching is a method that utilizes this characteristic to a great extent to promote the development of lateral buds; this method is, therefore, in harmony with the physiology of the plant.

To control the shape of bonsai, prevent the growth of terminal buds, and sometimes shorten the time required to increase the degree of precision in bonsai cultivation, branches can be dwarfed, shortened or replaced with branch buds.

The technique of nipping new or developing green buds is called pinching. Other methods include cutting over-long new buds to induce a second sprout and rubbing off undesired buds to retain only one bud on the branch.

For miscellaneous varieties such as Chinese elm, Japanese gray-bark elm, trident maple, and Japanese mountain maple, less fertilization and frequent pinching encourage the development of a fine tracery of branchlets. After one or two pinchings in spring, flowering and fruiting varieties can be allowed to grow without further pinching. When the flower buds are differentiated, remove any over-long branches according to the style desired.

Using a forceps plier to nip off newly sprouted leaf growth.

Leaf trimming

The removal of leaves at the tip of branches is called leaf trimming. Leaf trimming will help prevent the formation of long internodes and promote the growth of axillary buds. In addition, it ensures that all parts of the tree receive equal sunlight so that branches near the roots become thick and those at the top become finer. This allows the tree to grow much stronger. If sunlight cannot penetrate the foliage easily, ventilation will be poor. This may cause branches in the lower portion of the tree to weaken and the buds to be small. Gradually, the tree will lose vigor and grow withered branches and deformed leaves. In leaf trimming, keep one-third of the leaves on branches with fewer buds. On trees with an opposing arrangement of buds, leave only one leaf on each stem in order to change the growing direction. Frequent trimming is necessary to keep the foliage from becoming too dense, induce new shoots, and accelerate their metabolism.

The creation of a root-base

For the viewer, the appearance of the roots is an important factor in creating a sense of stability and age. Among bonsai growers, there is a popular saying that dictates "root-base first, trunk second, and branches third." A good root-base has thick roots that radiate horizontally and evenly from the trunk and are in close contact with the soil surface. Roots become more handsome as the tree ages. The age of the tree can thus be determined from the appearance of the root-base. To create good surface roots, it is necessary to plant the tree in a shallow container and make the soil surface higher than the rim of the pot. Plant the roots in such a way that they sit on the raised soil surface with some parts exposed and spreading outward in all directions; this will allow the roots to receive enough sunlight to grow quickly. If the tree material is raised from seed, it can be grown in a pot for one year and in the ground for another year. This will shorten the time of creation. Poor roots should be cut off or corrected as soon as possible because the growth of poor roots is intimately connected with the development of the branches. A tree with an even root-base will have balanced and uniform growth above ground; and its branches, foliage, and buds will look pleasing and neat.

Using short-bladed scissors to cut an overgrown branch tip.

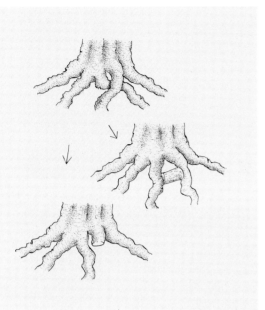

Use a piece of bamboo to shorten or spread curled root growth.

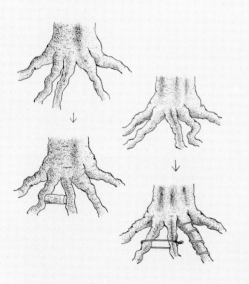

Use a piece of bamboo or wire to adjust entangled or crooked roots.

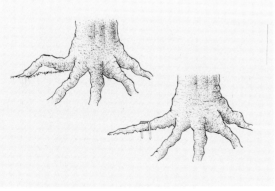

Use wire to station vertical root growth.

Correcting defects of roots

(1) Crooked, curled, entangled, or vertical roots can be severed or corrected with wires, pebbles, or pieces of bamboo. Vigorous stolons have to be cut short at the point where fine roots are growing as early as possible to ensure the even growth of fine roots.

(2) If there are roots, split downward-growing or thick roots to create new ones. Branches near the root-base can be layered, and huge roots can be split to compensate for an insufficiency of roots.

(3) Roots can also be created by height layering.

(4) Roots will thicken quickly when exposed to sunlight.

(5) A one-sided tree can be improved by root-grafting or seedling-grafting to form a twin-trunk or multi-trunk style. It can also be improved by covering bare root areas with fine pebbles or by inserting pebbles under floating roots.

(6) At points where roots are lacking, use a sharp knife or awl to remove the bark and cambium and expose the xylem. Then cover the wounds with sphagnum moss. Growing "sacrifice branches"— vigorous branches to be cut off later— above the wound can induce rooting. This method is especially effective in creating a shapely root-base in tree materials collected in the mountains.

How to produce a trunk

The trunk is the frame of the bonsai. It is thickest near the root-base and tapers toward the apex. The height of the tree should be 6 times the diameter of the trunk near the roots. This is an ideal proportion in bonsai creation. A desirable trunk should be thick near the root-base to display the illusion of stability and security. It should also have natural and fine lines and be without wounds.

How to make the trunk thick

(1) Choose a tree that has branches growing out at lower positions. Use a soil mix of coarse sand and clay particles and plant the tree in a large pot to make the roots thick. The branches will also become long and thick as a consequence. If some side branches right above the stock (the lower portion of the trunk) are left to grow freely, they will help to nurture the trunk.

(2) Fertilize the tree two or three times every month, particularly using nitrogenous fertilizers. The tree can be fertilized one month after transplanting. Roots must be trimmed before repotting.

(3) Suppress the growth of top branches to allow lower branches to elongate and the trunk to become thick. Top branches should also be trimmed and pinched.

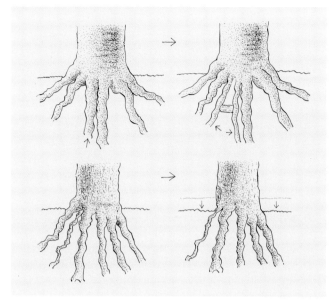

Use the correcting method to separate or redirect root growth.

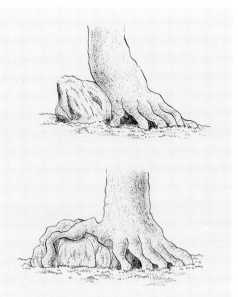

Alter a section of one-sided and floating roots by utilizing a stone.

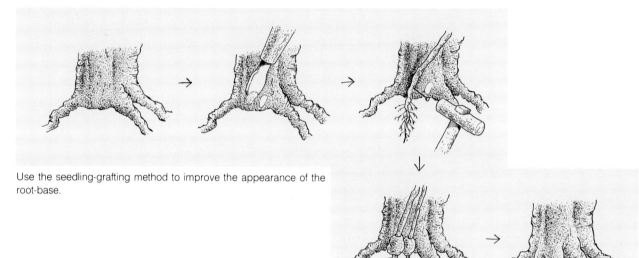

Use the seedling-grafting method to improve the appearance of the root-base.

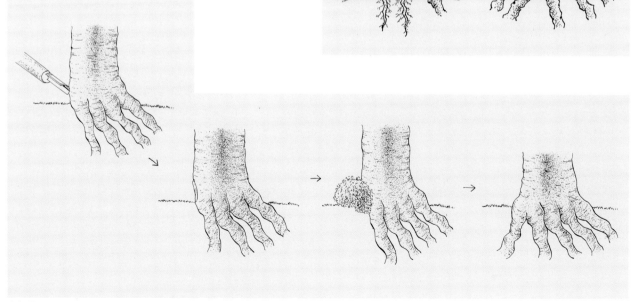

A knife or awl can be used to scar the trunk to stimulate new root growth.

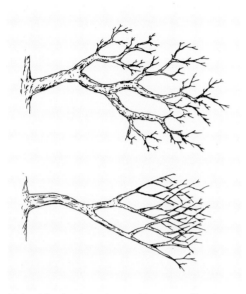

Natural flowing branches and less magnificent horned branches.

Observing the branch growth of natural trees aids in training branches.

How to create branches

Without a trunk, a tree can have no branches. Without branches, the tree will not develop a beautiful line. A tree looks powerful and massive if its branches and foliage are dense and fine. A goal in bonsai development is to recreate the beauty of aged trees. Branches should not be allowed to overhang one another or be too closely placed together or they will conceal the fine lines of the trunk. It is especially important to arrange carefully the points at which branches join the trunk. The total length of a branch from left to right should be 6 to 8 times the diameter of the trunk. Moreover, the diameter of a branch should not exceed 1/4 the diameter of its node. The small branches near the trunk may wither due to an insufficiency of sunshine, leaving only larger branches to survive. This characteristic must be taken into consideration in bonsai creation. The branches of old trees usually extend horizontally, while those of young trees shoot upward at an angle of 45 degrees. When trimming, leave some fine branchlets and extra branches to compensate for misjudgment.

Branches should be thick near the trunk and gradually become long and tapering toward the tip. There should be main and side branches, and the branching lines should be distinct, smooth, and natural. Never allow bifurcated branches or horned branches to grow on every tree species. The side branches should follow the curve and the flow of the main branches. The strength, flexibility, and space displayed by the trunk, branches, and foliage create beauty in the bonsai. To create the illusion of depth, position longer and more luxuriant branches to the rear. The major concern in arranging branches is to create space. Therefore, the size of the leaves and the amount of space should be carefully considered. There should not be too many vertical branches in a design. Deciduous trees, in particular, should exhibit the beauty of space even when they are in leaf because leaves are on the tree for a much longer time than they are off. If the number of branches is inadequate, inarching or grafting can be used to introduce new ones to improve the shape. In addition, trees like pines, trident maples, and Japanese gray-bark elms show apical dominance. If the lower branches are drastically pruned, new branches will not grow easily. Thus, special attention should be paid to branches lower on the trunk. For shrubs such as Satsuki azaleas, Taiwan fire-thorns and azaleas, branches toward the bottom are more vigorous and readily shoot new growth when pruned.

When creating a bonsai, study the tree carefully to discover its strong points. A good bonsai can be created by using training and shaping techniques suited to the tree's growing conditions.

Poor branches and their removal

Wheel branches: Certain varieties have several buds growing at one node, which later grow into whorled branches. If allowed to grow freely, these branches may cause the node to swell. Swollen nodes so damage the tree's appearance that it is necessary to retain only one suitable branch and remove the rest as soon as possible. When cutting off branches, leave the stumps on the tree and remove them after they wither. This is particularly important to prevent the formation of ugly nodes in pines.

Bar branches: In trees with an opposing arrangement of branches, two branches opposite each other will grow out at each node and the junction point will swell, thus detracting from the harmony of the design. It is therefore necessary to remove one of them.

Parallel branches: Trees with an alternating arrangement of branches sometimes grow two branches parallel to each other. In these cases, the lower branch will gradually weaken due to lack of sunlight. It is then necessary to remove one of the branches, according to the shape of the tree.

Upright branches: Spindling branches that grow vertically from a thick horizontal branch can weaken the parent branch because the terminal buds are the most vigorous. Upright branches can be removed or wired for correction.

Downward branches: Branchlets growing downward from a thick horizontal branch can cause poor ventilation and should be cut off as soon as possible.

One-sided branches: The shape of a tree with branches on only one side lacks stability and balance. Such a tree can, however, be used to create a wind-swept style.

Spindling branches: A branch that is too vigorous grows straight and fast and should be cut short or removed.

Crossing branches: If a main branch growing directly from the trunk crosses one of its branchlets, one of them should be removed.

Front-crossing branches: If a thick branch crosses the front of the trunk or passes from the front to the back, it should be cut short or removed.

Recurved branches: Branches that extend outward from the trunk and twist backwards should be shortened or cut off.

Front branches: Branches growing below the midway point of the tree on the front side and pointing toward the viewer will affect the line of the trunk and should be trained.

Because a tree growing in nature has not undergone pruning, the branches grow in a chaotic shape.

Poor Branches in Bonsai Creation:
(1) Wheel branch.	(7) Spindling branch.
(2) Bar branch.	(8) Crossing branch.
(3) Parallel branch.	(9) Front-crossing branch.
(4) Upright branch.	(10) Recurved branch.
(5) Downward branch.	(11) Front branch.
(6) One-sided branch.	

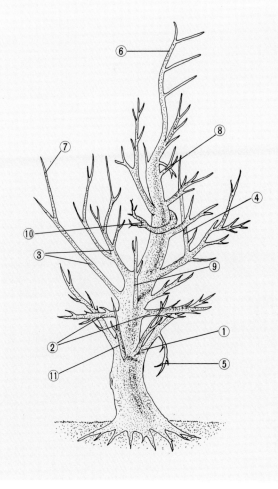

Pruning branch growth on a bonsai.

Training and leaf trimming on a bonsai.

Training and Wiring Tools:
(1) Wire pliers.
(2) Forked branch cutter.
(3) Wire cutter.
(4) Coarse branch shears.
(5) Small saw.
(6) Fine branch scissors.
(7) Forked branch cutter.
(8) Small saw.
(9) Medium-size branch shears.

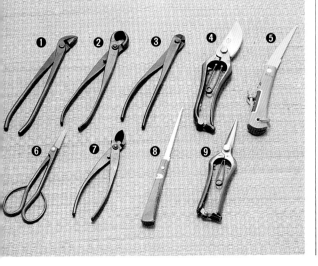

How to remove poor branches

Beginners should try to remove poor branches in two operations. In the first operation, cut the branch in the middle. In the second operation, remove the stump from the base of the branch. Avoid injuring other branches. Use a carving tool to hollow the cuts to prevent the formation of ugly swellings after healing. The cuts should also be treated with a tree sealant to accelerate healing, guard against bacteria, and prevent dehydration, which may cause the branches to rot or crack. Weak trees cannot stand drastic branch pruning, and the best times to remove branches are in spring, before the buds open, and in fall.

Wiring

Advantages of wiring

Wiring can change the growing direction of the trunk and branches. The curve and twist of the trunk and branches greatly enhance the line of the bonsai. Moreover, curves and twists narrow the food-conducting channels, and nutrition cannot reach the apical leaf surfaces easily, resulting in the decreased absorption of nitrogenous fertilizer and slow elongation of branches. Thus, the tree becomes stunted and aged. Surface tension, cell division, or reproduction occur in the part above the curve, while that part below the curve will develop thick tissues to secure the curve. The crown is the most vigorous part of the tree, and its growth can be suppressed by using wires to create a new apex. This will distribute the vigor to the lower branches. Establishing another apex contributes to both the physical and physiological dwarfing of the tree. Therefore, wiring is effective not only in shaping but also in promoting the differentiation of flower buds.

Suitable wiring time

It is preferable to wire trees in early spring when growth activity is slow because at that time the bark is supple and the branches are small and will not easily break if bent. Before the summer rainy season, as the flow of sap quickens, growth commences, and the trunk and branches start to build new tissues, cuts will heal more quickly. Removing the wire earlier may accelerate the growth of axillary buds. For deciduous varieties, the effects of shaping will be greater if wiring is done during the rainy season. Do not, however, apply wires to weak or newly repotted trees, especially after the rainy season when the flow of sap is fast and flexibility low; the tree may break easily when bent.

Entwined wire for training branches (Japanese gray-bark elm).

Entwined wire for training branches (Mulberry).

Types of metal wire for training branches.

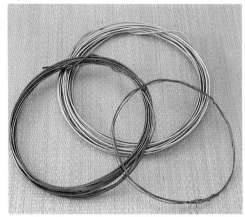

Procedures for wiring

Tools: Prepare a revolving stand, wire cutter, pliers, branch cutter, and carving knife.

Materials: Copper wire, aluminum wire, hemp cord, rubber board, iron rod, and straw. Zinc and iron wire will rust, and rust is difficult to remove, so avoid using them in wiring. Copper wire should be annealed in a fire of straw or newspaper. Copper wire becomes soft when heated and hard when bent; this property is very useful in wiring the tree. (Never use gas to anneal the copper wire because the gas will make it very hard and crisp.)

Fixing the tree: First of all, fix the tree firmly in the pot. If the tree is moved in the pot during wiring, the root-base may be injured and the corrected tree will tilt. Before wiring, the pot soil should be dry enough to prevent damage to the tree. Insert the wire in the soil and fix it firmly to prevent the soil-ball from breaking. If the moisture in a tree decreases, the branches become supple and hard to break, and the bark will not crack.

Determining shape: Put the tree on a revolving stand so that the midpoint of the tree is at eye level. Consider the features of the roots, trunk, and branches; choose the best side to be the front; and then determine what shape is suitable for the tree.

Disposition of foliage and branches: The guiding principle is to have the trunk and branches distinctly displayed. Branches growing from the front of the trunk block the view and should be removed. Try to retain branches at the rear to create depth and keep sacrifice branches to thicken the trunk. Branches growing below a point one-third up the tree's trunk must be removed.

Wiring: Wiring should be done from the roots to the apex, from lower branches to upper branches, and from thick branches to thin branches. Then apply a further adjustment of the wires from the apex to the lower branches.

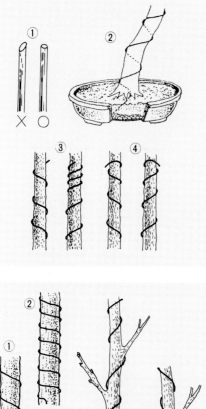

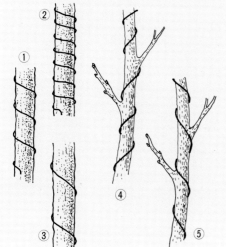

(1) Ideal spacing between wire windings.
(2) Spacing between wire windings that is too narrow.
(3) Spacing between wire windings that is too wide
(4) Counter-clockwise wiring.
(5) Clockwise wiring.

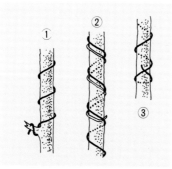

(1) An anchoring method wherein the end of the wire is fastened to a branch stump.
(2) An anchoring method wherein the end of the wire is secured under a turn of another wire.
(3) An anchoring method wherein the end of the wire is secured by looping back under the wire itself.

(1) Avoid producing a pointed tip when cutting the wire.
(2) Wind the wire around the trunk and bury the end in the soil for stability.
(3) If the end of the wire is not anchored firmly, windings around the trunk will loosen easily.
(4) Wire can be wound clockwise or counter-clockwise, but the end should be wound down the trunk.

Keys to good wiring

The wire must be secured: The end of the wire must be inserted into the soil to hold it in place. The first spiral must be firmly fixed before beginning the next. The last spiral must be fixed so that the wired part will not spring back to its original shape. The end of the wire should point downward slightly; otherwise, the bark may be injured by movement of the wire. The end of the wire should be cut evenly. Other branches can be used to aid training. If a wire is not long enough, two wires can be connected. The knot connecting two wires should not be visible from the front. Connection can be done by either inserting a new wire into the old one and securing it or screwing the two ends together.

Direction of the wire: The wire should spiral from right to left when right branches are being trained; similarly, the wire should spiral from left to right when left branches are being trained. If you want to change the direction of the wire when bending a branch, nearby branchlets can be used. The wire must pass around the outside edges of curved branches to prevent the branches from breaking.

Spacing between spirals: The wire should spiral at an angle of 45 degrees, and the spacing between spirals should not be too wide or too narrow. Use thicker wire to wire a thick trunk and thinner wire to wire a thin trunk.

Spacing between wire and bark: The wire should not be too tight or it may injure the bark; there should be a very narrow space left between the wire and the bark.

Wiring a thick trunk: When wiring a thick trunk, wrap the trunk with hemp-cord, rubber, or cloth. Hold the cortex and xylem firmly in place to avoid breakage and to protect the bark. Fasten two or three aluminum wires on the outside of the curve to increase flexibility. Then wire the trunk in a spiral pattern.

Wiring branches: When wiring branches, wire each branch alternately, that is, go from the first branch to the third or from the second branch to the fourth. The metal wire has to coil once around the trunk after each branch or the bending of one branch may affect another, and the correction of the bonsai will be altered. If a single branch is to be wired, the wire should be fixed in the bark at the point where the branches connect with the trunk. This will prevent the branch from breaking. Thick branches should be treated like thick trunks.

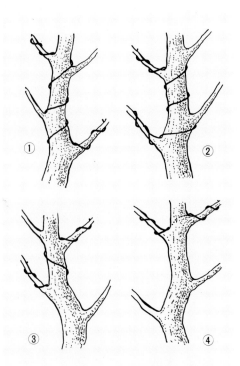

To prevent injury to the bark, wrap the wire with paper tape.

(1) Wrapping the wire from branch to branch on opposite sides of the trunk.
(2) Wrapping the wire from branch to branch on the same side of the trunk.
(3) Wrapping the trunk with just a single turn of wire is not effective.
(4) Training two branches by routing the wire across the trunk may result in choking one of the branches.

Using several wires: If two wires are used in wiring, they must be kept parallel to one another and never overlapped. This helps disperse surface tension.

Wiring several trunks: When wiring a multi-trunk style, it is best to start from the central trunk.

The best time to remove wires: The correct time for removing wires depends on the variety of the tree and its growing conditions. If the wire begins to penetrate the bark, it should be removed immediately. A wire cutter should be used to remove wires.

Bending and straightening techniques

The object of wiring is to bend or straighten the trunk or branches in order to change the curve, length, height, and angle of the tree. Through the technique of wiring, the bonsai grower can create a work of harmonious and unified beauty that expresses the bonsai's own particular style. Successful wiring is a key factor in determining whether a bonsai will ultimately become a fine work of art.

In bonsai wiring, bending and straightening are two very difficult techniques, which may be used to achieve creative expression in the bonsai. Bending and straightening are completely under the influence of the creator and dependent upon his experience, artistry, upbringing, and aesthetic taste. When practicing bending or straightening, pay attention to the following:

Bending: In addition to changing the line of the tree, bending has a shortening effect. When the trunk or branches are bent, the spirals of wire must not be too close or far apart and the wire itself must not be too thin. Otherwise, the fixing force may not be strong enough, and the wired trunk or branches may spring back to their former positions. If the spirals are too close to each other, the bending force may be so concentrated that the trunk or branches may break and the bark may crack. The wire must pass around the outside of the curve of the branch so that surface tension will be dispersed. Press the outside of the curve with the thumb or the palm of the hand and wind the wire slowly around the tree.

The rigidity of wire wrappings around a thick branch can be increased by placing two lengths of wire underneath for reinforcement.

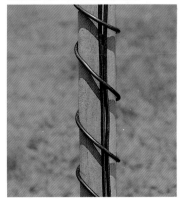

A completed wrapped wire overlapping reinforcement.

Widen the distance between two branches by using metal wire.

The distance between two branches can be decreased with a loop of metal wire, cushioned to protect the branches.

Another way to bring two branches closer together is to double and twist metal wire by using a third piece.

A broken branch resulting from the absence of wire wrapping.

A broken branch due to the failure to use both thumbs while bending the branch.

Pulling down branches: If a branch is to be bent downward, a hemp-cord must first be tied firmly around the node. Before adjusting the position of the branch, press the part below the node hard. This will prevent the branch from splitting from the trunk. This technique is very important in wiring a deciduous tree. When adjusting the thick branches of the black pine, cut two-thirds of the way through the branch and then wire the branch downward and fix it firmly. The cut will heal over naturally and quickly if treated with a sealant. If some weight is also placed on the branch, the results of bending will be better.

Avoid repetitive bending and straightening: Before any operation, plan the design first and follow the required steps one by one. Do not bend or straighten the branch repeatedly; this may cause the cortex to separate from the xylem or the xylem tissue to swell and form unsightly lumps. This phenomenon often occurs in the pine and juniper.

Drastic bending: If you have difficulty bending a thick branch, you can use a pair of pliers to hold the wire or an iron rod or adjusting device, such as a clamp or jack, to alter the direction of the branch. The force will increase if the distance between the fulcrum and the point of the application of the force is also increased. Before bending the branch, test the adjusting device. Then bend the branch to the desired position carefully and slowly to prevent breakage.

(1) A hanging weight may be used to bend a branch.
(2) One end of the wire can be fastened to the bonsai container to train a trunk to grow vertically.
(3) Wire can be anchored to the trunk to force horizontal branch growth.
(4) Wire can be wrapped around the branch and trunk to bend a branch.

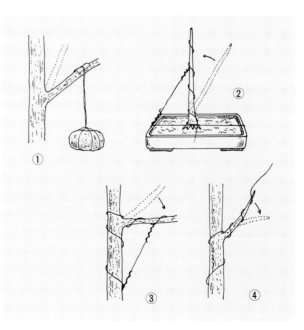

Adjusting thick branches: This is the most difficult technique in wiring and should be done cautiously. If, however, you apply the principle of the lever ingeniously and use tools to aid bending, the desired effect may be achieved with less effort. First wrap the tree with hemp-cord, rubber, or cloth. Hold the cortex and xylem firmly in place to prevent their separation. When using an adjuster, make sure that the part of the branch to be clamped is wrapped with a thick rubber cushion. When the branch or trunk is bent to the desired position, wire the tree and remove the instrument so that the bark will not be damaged by concentrated pressure. Before removing the adjuster, fix the angle of the bend with wires to prevent branches from rebounding. At first, try to bend the tree only slightly; wait one month or two for the wood to soften before readjusting the position. This technique requires patience, and several operations are necessary to achieve the purpose.

Straightening thick branches: It takes less effort to straighten the branches if an iron rod is used; but the branches must be protected by rubber cushions.

As wiring can drastically suppress the growth of the tree, it is necessary to apply fertilizers in advance. Except for some necessary curved branches and downward branches, try to have all the branches grow at an upward angle. The end of downward branches and the tail of a cascade should be adjusted to grow upward to increase tree vigor and prevent withering. The line of the branchlets should vary according to the pattern of the parent branches which, in turn, should vary according to the line of the trunk, making the overall shape harmonious. If a branch has a slight split, it should be fixed, treated with sealant, and tied firmly with hemp-cord or cloth. Branches must be wired from the point where they meet the trunk, and the curves should have variety. However, avoid very drastic bending, or the tree will look unnatural. Branches should start from the outside of a curve so that the resulting design displays a sense of perspective.

Maintenance after wiring

Wiring is a difficult operation in creating a bonsai. It is also the decisive factor in determining whether a bonsai is artistically successful. Because the trunk and branches are bent in wiring, the water- and nutrition-conducting channels become narrower. The cells in the cortex, cambium, and xylem can be damaged severely when thick branches are wired. Therefore, the tree should be carefully guarded against dehydration.

When conductive channels are affected, water and nutrition absorbed by the roots cannot reach the leaf surface easily, and there may be a supply insufficient for photosynthesis. Therefore, it is essential to spray water on the leaves, branches, and trunk frequently to supply additional moisture. In addition, avoid placing the bonsai in intense sunlight. Place it in a damp and semi-shady place. The bonsai needs good ventilation, but make sure it is not exposed to strong winds; otherwise, water will evaporate very quickly. Also, pay special attention to daily watering. If the soil is too wet, the roots may rot; but if the soil is too dry, the tree will not get enough moisture. Try to maintain the tree by following the same procedures for caring for a transplanted and repotted tree.

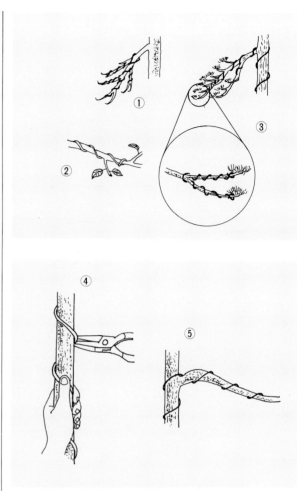

(1) The ends of the lower branches of deciduous varieties should be wired to grow upwards.
(2) Wire wrapped around the tip of a branch can be fixed by wrapping the end of the wire backwards.
(3) Use wire to train the new upward branch growth of a pine tree.
(4) Use a needle nose plier being for winding wire on a thick trunk.
(5) Excessive wire application can cause a bulge to grow on a trained branch.

Use an adjustment device to bend a thick trunk.

TRANSPLANTING
AND REPOTTING TECHNIQUES

Root Pruning and Washing:
(1) When repotting bonsai, use water to wash the roots.
(2) Prune the thick roots.
(3) The root clump after completion of pruning.

Transplanting and Repotting Techniques

A bonsai can continue growing in a limited amount of soil for several decades, or even hundreds of years, and remain vigorous and luxuriant. The secret of achieving such long life is repotting. Repotting is considered the most important task in bonsai cultivation because it helps to control the number and growth of roots.

A bonsai is grown within the confines of a pot; if it is not repotted at regular intervals, it will suffer injuries. The following is a discussion of possible injuries and the purposes of repotting.

A bonsai will become rootbound and the roots will age

The roots of plants grow constantly throughout the night in order to absorb moisture and nutrients. If the pot is full of roots, the air in the soil will decrease in proportion. (There should be a balanced proportion of soil, water, and air.) If roots or root waste fill the soil pores, the solid structure of the soil will be damaged and hinder aeration, which results in a deficiency of oxygen, smaller soil pores, decreased water retention, and poor drainage. The pressure caused by growing roots will have the same effect. Such changes in bonsai soil can retard plant growth; furthermore, if old roots fill the pot, the overall root-system will age and gradually lose vigor. New roots will then be unable to grow, and the amount of water and nutrient absorption will also drop drastically. Foliage and branches will subsequently lose vigor or wilt. The only way to save the bonsai is to repot it and cut out old fibrous and thick roots, to check expansion of undesirable roots, and to induce the growth of fine roots from the cuts. This will help the tree recover its health, prevent the formation of long internodes, and help the tree retain its shape. In general, when repotting a tree, the proportion of roots to be pruned should be: 1/3 – 1/2 of the root-system of a tree being trained and 1/4 – 1/3 of the root-system of an established bonsai.

In brief, the purpose of repotting is to control the size and expansion of the root-system. Moreover, repotting offers an opportunity to study the root-system and detect pest or disease damage. One characteristic of growing plants in pots is that they are easy to control and look after; effectively managed, this characteristic can become a superb technique in bonsai cultivation.

Bonsai soil will age

If a bonsai is not repotted, its soil will undergo physical and chemical deterioration.

Physical deterioration: If left unrepotted, the roots of the tree will fill the pot and create pressure, breaking down the crumbly structure of granular soil, which is necessary to retain moisture and aid the respiratory process of the root-system. Constant daily watering, freezing in winter, pressure created by growing roots, and decreased porosity due to age and organic waste matter all contribute to make soil aeration poor. Capillary pores will also become clogged and impede drainage, which can cause root decay.

Chemical deterioration: If the proportion of microelements in the soil is inadequate, the soil will acidify. Because Taiwan has plenty of rainfall, carbon dioxide in the air readily dissolves in rainwater to form carbonic acid. Calcium also dissolves readily in water to form carbon bicarbonate. This drains away with daily watering, making the soil acid. (Of course, there are some species of trees that do well with acid soil, e.g. Satsuki azaleas.) Daily watering and regular fertilizing also help to accelerate the process of acidification.

Transplanting to improve aesthetic effect

Tree materials are first grown in unglazed containers. After being well cultivated, they can be transplanted to decorative pots. Thus, the color, shape, and size of the pot may be chosen to harmonize and complement the tree to create a pleasing overall design

Transplanting and repotting to prevent pests

Pests lay eggs in the soil and damage it. If pest attacks on roots are ignored, the bonsai will be injured. Repotting then becomes necessary. During repotting, roots should be washed clean. Rotten and sick roots must be cut away and soaked in a 1:1000 diluted zinc manganese disinfectant to kill germs.

Bonsai that have not been repotted for a long time easily become weak.

The old roots of the planted tree are long and fill the entire container.

Following repotting, an attractive bonsai container has been substituted.

Transplanting and Repotting Procedures (Formosan hackberry):
(1) Cut the wire holding the plant in the container.
(2) Use a blade to separate the soil and root mass from the inside of the container.
(3) Tap the container lightly to loosen the soil.

Root-pruning and repotting to maintain shape

The growth of the roots is proportionate to the growth of the foliage and branches above ground. If some branches develop long internodes, part of the root-system also elongates. If there are long and thick roots, the tree will also produce long and thick branches or send out adventitious buds despite trimming, which damage the overall shape of the bonsai. For this reason, repotting is necessary to remove old roots and induce fine roots to grow so that a fine structure can be formed and the quality of the tree improved.

In general, trees being trained are grown in coarse granular soil. Coarse soil has large pore spaces and good aeration, and roots can thicken easily in it, increasing the tree's vigor. Granular soil with finer particles is suitable for established bonsai because the pore space is small. Soil changes can help to develop fine roots, branchlets, and shorten internodes. Thus, repotting helps maintain the shape of the bonsai.

How often to repot the tree

Generally, the roots of trees being trained grow faster. Pines and junipers should be repotted yearly or once every other year. Miscellaneous varieties should be repotted yearly. For established bonsai and miscellaneous varieties, repotting should be done once every two or three years, and pines and junipers once every three or five years.

The frequency of repotting also varies greatly with the species. Trees that produce fine roots vigorously should be repotted within a shorter period of time. Satsuki azaleas, for instance, will lose vigor if the roots in the pot become entangled. It is preferable to repot them after flowering. Other flowering and fruiting varieties should be repotted yearly or once every other year.

Suitable seasons for repotting

There is no definite rule about repotting seasons that is applicable to all species. Repotting time varies with species, age, climatic zone, weather, rainfall, and purpose.

As a rule, frigid zone trees should be repotted when buds begin to sprout, and deciduous trees 15 days before spring buds open; this is at the end of the deciduous tree's dormant season, when it is full of vigor. If they are damaged during repotting, they recuperate quickly at this time. Trees that sprout early should be repotted early; conversely, trees that bud late should be repotted late.

Temperate varieties—such as common pomegranates, Chinese hackberries, cape gardenias, Fukien teas, banyans, Chinese podocarpuses, common jasmin oranges, box-trees, dwarf kumquats, common cryptomerias, and needle junipers—should be repotted in March and April when temperatures are higher.

There is a saying in China about bamboo: "Plant bamboo before Tomb-Sweeping Day." The optimum time for repotting or separating bamboo is ten days before or after Tomb-Sweeping Day, which falls on April 5 in the Chinese lunar calendar.

Some plants— such as flowering quinces, flowering cherries, apples, Japanese flowering apricots, and Japanese flowering quinces— are liable to suffer from root knots if repotted in spring when the temperature begins to rise. At this time the rate of infection is high and disease microbes may enter through the wounds. It is best to repot these species in fall or winter.

When roots have filled the pot, some will come out through the drainage holes. By examining the bottom of the pot, it is easy to tell whether or not the tree needs repotting. After drastic pruning, it is necessary to repot the tree; do not, however, repot the tree before or after wiring. When repotting a tree, both the root-system and branches require trimming, and the severed branches can be used for cuttings. It is convenient if repotting time corresponds with the season for planting cuttings.

Procedures for repotting

In order to avoid wasting time looking for materials during repotting, which may cause fine roots to dry up, it is necessary to prepare the following materials before the operation: (1) soil mixture, (2) tools, (3) plastic mesh, (4) revolving stand, and (5) aluminum wire. In addition, choose a fine and windless day (avoid strong winds and hot sun) for repotting. Then follow the step by step repotting guidelines.

Removing the tree from the pot

Before repotting, reduce the amount of water given to the plant so that it is dry enough to facilitate removal of old soil. For pots with a narrow base and a wide top, first cut the aluminum wire that holds the tree in place, then hammer the edge of the pot with your fists slightly. The vibration will cause the soil to separate from the pot, making it easier to remove the tree. For pots with a wide body and a narrow top or of uniform width, use a sharp knife to cut along the edge of the soil, and lift the tree out. Another alternative is to loosen the soil slowly along the edge of the pot until the soil slides out of the mouth of the pot easily. Use a stick to push the soil out of the bottom of the pot from the drainage holes. This must be done with great care to prevent damaging the root-system and the container.

Root pruning

First of all, cut long and aged roots from the outer portion of the soil. Use a chopstick to slowly remove all the old soil. Next, wash the roots thoroughly with water so that their skins are revealed. The root-system must then be carefully examined and cared for.

Sick roots: Root knots often occur in the roots of flowering quinces and Japanese flowering quinces. If root knots are detected, the affected roots must be completely removed. Repotting of these varieties is best done between fall and winter; the trees are likely to suffer from root knots if repotted in spring.

(4) Carefully remove the tree.
(5) Remove the soil from the roots.
(6) Prune the old roots.

(7) Place plastic mesh over the drainage holes of the container.
(8) Install the wires that are to hold the plant in the container.
(9) Add the bottom layer of coarse soil particles.
(10) Add the center layer of medium-size particles, with the layer slightly higher in the center.

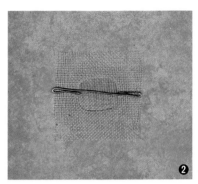

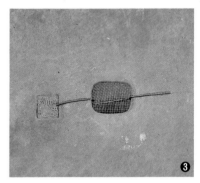

(1) How the mesh over the drainage holes is fastened.
(2) View of the inner surface of the container.
(3) View of the bottom of the container.

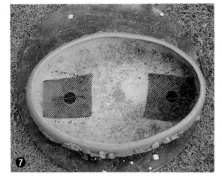

(11) Position the tree in the container and level off the roots.
(12) Fasten the tree to the container with wires.
(13) Fill the container with soil and pack it in with a bamboo stick.
(14) Water the tree thoroughly; this is the final step in repotting.

Decayed roots: Study the condition of the roots when they are repotted. Cut away injured or rotten roots to encourage the growth of new roots.

Adventitious roots: Fine roots growing at undesirable angles from a handsome root-base may thicken and decrease the beauty of the root-system. It is necessary to prune them as soon as possible to ensure an even root-base.

Downward roots: Strong and downward roots should be cut to improve the growth of a radial root-system and to strengthen the growth of branches.

Recurved roots: If neglected, roots that twist back upon themselves can intertwine with other roots and form an entangled root-system, detracting from the beauty of the root-base. They should be cut off. If there are not enough roots and recurved roots are needed, they should be separated from each other with pieces of wood or pebbles to adjust the direction of their growth.

Vertical roots: Roots that jut out vertically from a handsome root-base are very unpleasing in a bonsai planted in a shallow pot; they should be removed.

Straight roots: Roots are characteristically geotropic. If they are too vigorous, they may affect the growth of other roots and, should, therefore, be cut off. In general, roots at an angle of more than 45 degrees from the base of the tree should be completely removed. The tree can then be potted in a shallow pot to form an aesthetically pleasing bonsai.

Thick roots: Thick roots can weaken good branching roots and should be cut off from the base of the tree. If there are no good roots, thick roots can be shortened and trimmed to send out fine branch roots, or they can be cut into halves and separated by pebbles or pieces of wood.

Roots should be cut on a slant with the cut facing downward. Use a sharp knife to make cuts even to prevent rotting and accelerate healing. The roots should then be wrapped with sphagnum moss to prevent dehydration, which can affect rooting.

Procedures for transplanting

(1) First of all, prepare a pot of suitable shape, size, and color.

(2) Cover the drainage holes with plastic mesh to prevent loss of soil, and fasten the mesh with aluminum wire.

(3) Prepare a good soil mix that is compatible with the tree species and the size of the pot. Cover the bottom of the pot with a layer of coarse soil particles that can provide good aeration and good drainage. The tree should be positioned slightly off center so that the roots and soil are in close contact and the stock is above the level of the pot rim.

Coarse, powerful roots reflect the movement of the plant.

Using the layering method to create a new root-base.

The beautiful root-base one year after the application of the layering method.

245

A naturally occurring hanging root growth.

(4) Plant the pruned tree in a suitable position. Make sure that the front of the bonsai is aligned correctly. Extend the roots outward as much as possible. Tie the tree to the pot with aluminum wire. Spread another layer of medium-sized soil particles on top. Use a chopstick to prod between roots so that soil particles are in close contact with the roots.

(5) Finally, fill the pot with fine topsoil and level it. The level of the soil around the edge of the pot should be lower than the edge to prevent water or liquid fertilizers from overflowing. Freshly repotted soil is loose and must be covered with moss or sphagnum moss. In addition to preventing the loss of soil, moss can also impart a feeling of stability and add variety to the soil surface.

(6) After repotting, water the tree sufficiently to wash away fine clay particles, until the water coming through the drainage holes is clear. Put the repotted tree in a shady, damp, and well-aired position. Spray the leaves frequently until new roots appear. Do not fertilize the tree for one month.

The propagation of moss

(1) Moss grown in woods, courtyards, or damp areas can be directly transplanted to bonsai soil. Before any moss is planted, however, it is necessary to remove the soil attached to it.

(2) Used soil mixture can be stored in a wooden box and moss added to it. Put the box in a shady place and water frequently. Very soon there will be a luxuriant growth of moss.

(3) Dry moss in the sun. After transplanting and repotting, sprinkle moss and shredded sphagnum moss on the soil surface. A covering of moss will soon grow.

(4) When watering, apply starch (water in which rice has been washed) or superphosphate to the soil or stones to induce moss growth.

(5) Used moss that has been removed can be grown in old bonsai soil.

Moss increases the beauty of the tree, prevents the loss of soil, helps the plant resist cold temperatures, and preserves moisture. There are many types, shapes, and colors of moss. If various types, heights, and colors of moss are used in a planting, the bonsai will be full of variety.

Green Moss Propagation Method:
(1) Collect green moss.
(2) Prepare the planting bed.
(3) Remove the soil on the bottom of the moss.
(4) Transplant the moss to the planting bed.

THE CREATION OF JINNS
AND SHARIES

A dragon juniper bonsai with a naturally formed shari.

The Creation of Jinns and Sharies

Old trees growing in the wild have long been subjected to the forces of nature. After being struck by lightning and ravaged by strong winds, rain, frost, snow, fallen boulders, and diseases, the crown or some branches on old trees may wither up and the bark fall off, exposing the silvery xylem. If the bark is pulled off at the tips of the branch or the apex, the resulting part is called a "jinn"; if part of the trunk's bark is stripped off, it is called a "shari."

Because emphasis has been placed on preserving the environment, tree materials with natural jinns and sharies are becoming rare. But because the art of bonsai has progressed from simply growing potted trees to creating handsome works of art, bonsai lovers can try to imitate nature and create artificial jinns and sharies. As a general rule, the pine and juniper, whose wood is hard and does not easily decay, are used. To create a jinn, a withered or superfluous branch is specially treated and its bark peeled off; to create a shari, part of the trunk is barked so that trunk canals twist and wind round the trunk. Other species of trees with loose and soft xylem may be created into artificial jinns or sharies, but they will not last long and may become a major defect in the tree.

Jinning is now a widely applied technique in bonsai creation because it can greatly increase the beauty of a tree. The silvery color of driftwood forms a pleasing contrast to foliage and bark; it can also create more space in the design, add to the effect of depth and antiquity, and give variety to the line of trunk and branches. This technique emphasizes the mysterious quality of turning wastes into treasures. The value of the bonsai with a jinn or shari also increases. Using jinns and sharies reinforces the antiquity of trees and can produce impressive results.

Determining the frontal orientation

Selecting the side of the tree that will serve as the front is very important in the creation of bonsai. Whether a bonsai is trained, wired, repotted, or jinned, it is necessary to identify the front of the trunk before any step is taken; otherwise, regardless of the superiority of creative technique, the design will never be perfectly consistent and harmonious.

Naturally deformed Sargent junipers imparting a feeling of wildness.

There are three characteristics to look for when choosing the front of the tree: (1) the width of the surface roots and trunk from left to right; (2) the most prominent curve of the trunk; (3) the side on which the apex leans slightly forward. Some trunk canals should be visible on the front of the trunk. They must twist and wind up the tree along with the white shari. If only shari is visible from the front, the viewer cannot feel the spirit of the tree struggling valiantly for survival.

Plan the design carefully

The peeling of bark is a serious challenge for the creation of jinns and sharies because mistakes cannot be mended. Different species of trees along with varying sizes of branches and trunks present a vast spectrum of hardness, flexibility, and elasticity. Therefore, before working on the tree, think about the overall design and carefully select the part of the tree to be jinned. Try to retain the natural grain of the wood. Never be hasty or rash in making a jinn or shari; the damage may be irreparable.

First use chalk to mark the direction of the trunk canal, showing how it twists and at what angle. This is important because the line of the trunk canal has considerable influence on the shape of the bonsai.

Do not leave only one trunk canal or it will thicken after a period of time and separate from the shari. It is better to keep at least two trunk canals.

When there are two trunk canals, they should be positioned on either side of the front of the trunk so that the front can continue to thicken; when there are three trunk canals, one should be at the back of the trunk, forming a slanting triangle.

Finally, cut the trunk canals clearly with a sharp knife. The cut must be even to allow the wound to cure and swell easily. At first leave the trunk canals wide. After they swell, make them narrower to reveal the layers of the trunk surface. Leaves on a branch to be jinned should be removed beforehand. Use a pair of pliers and patiently peel the bark off to the xylem. With careful carving, a natural and beautiful jinn or driftwood can be created.

A bonsai with one trunk canal preserved.

A bonsai with two trunk canals preserved.

A bonsai with three trunk canals preserved.

The swollen appearance of a trunk canal.

Diagram of the Proper Placement of Trunk Canals.

Jinn and Shari Creation Procedures (Sargent juniper):
(1) Select the ideal site.
(2) Scrape the bark off the site with a bronze-bristle brush.
(3) Use chalk to draw a line to site the trunk canal.
(4) Strip the bark to produce a jinn.
(5) Gouge the trunk canal.
(6) The completed jinn and shari.
(7) The completed work, after sculpting and shaping

After stripping the bark, use metal wire to shape the branch.

Some guidelines in creation

(1) Jinning should never be done on a newly transplanted and repotted tree because the mechanisms of its roots will not have completely recovered and the tree may wither.

(2) The xylem of young trees and ground-planted trees is not hard enough and may decay easily, so it is best to grow them in pots for three to five years, attempting to produce jinns or sharies on them. It is advisable to adjust the branches before peeling any bark. Then use metal wire to adjust the shape of the trunk or branches. Variations in the length, width, angle and shape of jinns are necessary to make the style of the trunk unique.

(3) It is preferable to use a branch with many fine branchlets to create jinns; the tree will look more attractive.

(4) The trunk canal should never spiral horizontally up the trunk. This not only is unnatural and ugly but also affects growth.

(5) Choose a vigorous tree when creating trunk canals. The best time for this operation is between March and May when the flow of sap is more active and the cuts can be healed and swell more easily. However, carving should be done in winter when the flow of sap is slow. Do not carve the tree in the hot summer season because the operation may harm the tree's growth. After creating trunk canals, it is necessary to water the foliage and put the tree in a shady place.

(6) Never apply lime-and-sulphur solution before the xylem is thoroughly dry (which requires at least one month). Cuts along the trunk canal should be left untreated before they heal over or the solution may enter the cuts and kill the tree.

An electric sculpting tool.

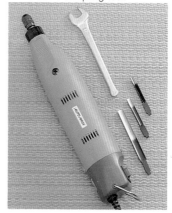

Various sculpting handtools.

An electric sculpting tool.

The operation of carving jinns and sharies

There are three stages in carving or sculpting jinns and sharies: rough carving, finished carving, and polished carving. The line of the carving should follow the direction of the wood fiber. Try to preserve brown, hard wood and remove white, loose parts to the extent possible.

Rough carving: Use a saw, a chisel, and an awl to make holes or grooves.

Finish carving: Use an electric drill to finish off the jinn or shari, carving tiny holes and fine grooves.

Polish carving: Polish the finished jinn or shari to remove traces of artificiality; try to make it look natural and beautiful.

A naturally jinned and sharied Japanese premna.

A man-made jinned and sharied Sargent juniper.

A naturally sharied Taiwan sageretia.

A vigorously growing bonsai will have a trunk canal that swells easily.

Brush off moss or fungal growths on trunk.

Apply a solution of lime and sulphur.

The maintenance of jinns and sharies

The grandeur and gracefulness of jinns and sharis, the feeling of antiquity and fortitude they impart, stimulate the imagination. Naturally occurring jinns and sharies have a hard texture, and it is necessary to choose trees with hard wood to create artificial jinns and sharies, so that they may be preserved for a long time.

Because bonsai are placed outdoors and are subjected to rain and wind as well as daily watering, dampness may cause jinns and sharies to decay. The following points should be observed:

Cleansing: Because jinns and sharies are not protected by bark and are exposed to the air, fungi and pollution are major reasons for decay. It is, therefore, necessary to wash and clean jinns and sharies in spring and fall. Since Taiwan has a humid climate and an abundance of rainfall, cleansing is particularly important.

Dryness: Dampness is the chief cause of fungi. Watering and rain can wet jinns and sharies; therefore, sunlight and fresh air must be readily available and the dampness of the topsoil carefully monitored. The decay of jinns and sharies usually starts near the surface soil.

Care: Jinns and sharies should be treated with chemical compounds after they are cleansed and dried. First, apply a quick-drying glue to increase hardness and prevent water penetration. Then treat them with PCP or lime-and-sulphur. Better results can be achieved if this is done before the rainy season in spring and early summer and after every rainfall.

The jinned and sharied bonsai after treatment.

CHOOSING THE POT

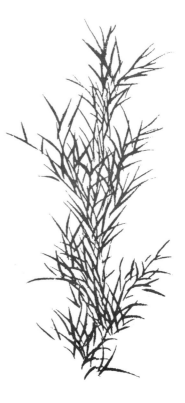

A multicolor six-sided container and an ancient oblong container, both of the Ch'ing Dynasty.

Ancient square containers from Shihwan, Canton.

A bonsai container that is too large (Taiwan fire-thorn).

Choosing the Pot

Bonsai is a form of landscaping that uses trees and rocks as the subject. The selection of the pot is important because it allows the viewer to imagine the potted tree growing in its natural environment. The pot is one of the three essential elements that constitute a bonsai. If a fine tree is planted in an unsuitable pot, it will look unpleasing and lack stability and harmony, or the pot may become the dominant element and detract from the overall beauty of the design. If the choice of the pot and the means of positioning the tree are appropriate, tree and pot will complement each other. Thus, the depth of the bonsai in the pot, the planting position, and the proportion of the tree to the size, color, shape, height, and width of the pot are closely related to the message the artist wants to convey.

Harmony between the size of the tree and the pot

The ideal proportion of the width of the pot is 2/3 to 3/4 of the height of the tree, and the depth should be about 1/2 of the height of the tree. The height of the pot should be equivalent to the diameter of the trunk. These proportions are best to display harmony and stability.

Generally speaking, large trees should be grown in large pots, small trees in small pots. Sometimes a small tree may be planted in a large pot and then embellished with fine rocks, ornaments, and a little landscaping of the soil surface to create a whimsical feeling. Conversely, a large tree may sometimes be grown in a smaller pot to heighten the feeling of loftiness and dominance. In addition, for certain species that require more water, it is preferable to use larger or higher pots for better growth.

Harmony between the color of the tree and the pot

Though the tree is the main element in bonsai creation, the pot is a supporting one. Thus, the color of the pot is very important and should not detract from the beauty of the tree. In general, bright contrasting colors or soft harmonizing colors should be chosen. Reddish pots look wild and strong and can express the character of rocky mountains or barren lands; blue is associated with water; yellow implies golden leaves and autumn scenes; green suggests the verdure of a meadow. For pines and junipers, it is best to use plain unglazed pots of austere color, such as dull red, reddish, purple, or brownish-red Yihsing wares or nanman wares. For flowers and fruits, pots with bright colors, such as light yellow, crimson, or dark green earthenware, celadon, nanman, or shiro kochi can be chosen to heighten the beauty of the bonsai.

A papaya-shaped container.

An oval drum container.

An old Japanese oblong container in imitation of a Chinese container.

A drum-shaped container.

Ancient oblong and round containers.

Ancient containers with flared mouths from Shihwan, Canton.

A variety of containers for super miniature bonsai.

Harmony in the shape of the tree and the pot

The shape of the pot suggests various kinds of terrain. Deep pots suggest overhanging cliffs and precipices and are suitable for cascades. Semi-deep pots carry the feeling of hillocks and are suitable for slanting styles. Shallow pots represent extensive plains and should be chosen for group plantings and upright styles because they help to reinforce the illusion of massiveness.

Quadrilateral pots imply undulating terrain and are ideal for strong and dominant varieties such as pines and junipers. Round pots suggest tender beauty and can be appreciated from all angles; they are suitable for flowering trees and grasses. Rectangular pots have distinct sides and a front and display the feeling of high mountains; they are suitable for strong and imposing trees. Oval pots represent riverside and lakeside scenes and are suitable for the soft and light styles of miscellaneous varieties.

Positioning the tree in the container

In order to exhibit a pleasing shape, the tree should not be placed in the center of the pot. More space is necessary on the side with a lean or with heavy branches. Trees leaning to the right should have more space on the right. Trees leaning to the left should have more space on the left. It is best to keep a ratio of 4 to 6 or 3 to 7 when positioning a tree in a pot. The degree of the slant of the tree and the height of mounds on the soil surface influence the visual effect. It is best to plant the tree a little higher than the soil surface and expose some part of the root so that the surface roots can obtain sufficient sunlight to thicken and age. Make the soil around the edge of the pot slightly lower than the soil in the center so that water and fertilizer can flow toward the edge of the pot and be absorbed by the roots. The temperature of soil is highest at the edges, and roots there are the most abundant and vigorous.

Guidelines for choosing pots and containers

(1) Pay attention to the inner shape of the pot to make sure it is even, porous, and delicate. The drainage holes should be at the lowest part of the bottom and able to provide good drainage.

(2) The container must be fine, without flaws and cracks, and the bottom should be able to rest firmly on a level surface.

(3) If the container has 3 legs, one of them must face the front. For slanting or cascade styles, one of the legs should support the side of the lean so that the tree will not be blown over in strong winds.

(4) Nanman pots or irregular containers have uneven rims. Try to position the lower rim so that it faces the front.

(5) Consider whether calligraphy, painting, or flawed glazes on the pot are appropriate on the front.

(6) Old pots should be cleaned and sterilized in the sun before being used.

(7) Match old trees with old pots and young trees with new pots, to emphasize the age or youth of the bonsai.

A tall square container hand-made out of clay.

The planting position of a coiled-style bonsai in a container.

The planting position of a cascade-style bonsai in a container.

The planting position of an informal upright-style bonsai in a container.

The planting position of a slanting-style bonsai in a container.

The planting position of an upright-style bonsai in a container.

The planting position of a group-planting style bonsai in a container.

The planting position of a broom-style bonsai in a container.

The planting position of a tree in an oval container.

The tree planted at the left side of a container lacks sufficient space.

The planting position of a tree in a round container.

The tree planted at the right side of a container creates a sense of instability.

The planting position of a tree in an oblong container.

The planting position of a tree in a square container.

The proper planting position of a tree leaning to the right.

MINIATURE BONSAI

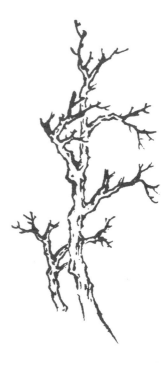

A room with an interior decoration of super miniature bonsai.

An art studio decorated with super miniature bonsai.

Miniature Bonsai

Miniature bonsai are bonsai that measure between 6 in. and 8 in. Bonsai below 6 in. are called super miniature bonsai and those between 8 in. and 12 in. are called small bonsai. Although miniature bonsai do not attain the aura of age and refinement that characterize medium and large bonsai, they are delicate, lovely, and possess interesting characteristics in their own right. Despite their small size, miniature bonsai can be used to display the beauty of many tree species and bring great pleasure to their owners.

Reasons for their popularity

With today's tremendous increases in population, living space in cities is steadily shrinking. In such crowded environments, miniature bonsai are ideal for enjoyment because they occupy little space; over a hundred miniature bonsai can be grown on a roof or balcony. The materials used to create miniature bonsai are also not as expensive as those used to grow medium or large bonsai and will, therefore, cause the novice less distress if the creation fails. Tree materials can be easily obtained by growing from seed, cutting, or height layering, and these can be trained into miniature bonsai in a very short time. Unlike medium and large bonsai, which often take decades to establish, miniature bonsai can be grown into handsome specimens in three to five years. In addition, their small size allows them to be moved and placed anywhere—in the living room, near the door, on a table or a stand. Thus, they can become a part of everyday life and add vitality to the environment. Finally, it is also easy to care for miniature bonsai. These characteristics explain miniature bonsai's rapid development at home and abroad and popularity with young and old alike.

The concept of creation

Because of their tiny size and height, it is necessary to remove superfluous branches and foliage when a miniature bonsai is trained. The overall design of the tree must be simple in order to emphasize the bonsai's uniqueness and to distill the tree to an elemental form whose meaning is readily recognizable.

Care of miniature bonsai

Since a miniature bonsai is grown in a tiny container and watered daily, its soil becomes acid more easily than that of a larger

A shelf display for the appreciation of miniature bonsai.

bonsai. If the soil is too acid, microelements such as boron and magnesium will undergo chemical changes, become insoluble and gradually diminish. A little lime can be applied to the soil to compensate for this deficiency; but the amount must be just right because over-application of lime can make the soil alkaline and manganese insoluble, causing chlorosis. Therefore, testing soil acidity is necessary; frequent repotting and transplanting are also the best means to prevent acidification.

Appreciating miniature bonsai

The basic principles for appreciating miniature bonsai do not differ very much from those for evaluating medium or large bonsai. The beauty of the overall design as well as the individual form of the roots, trunk, branches, and crown must be taken into consideration. The table surface, pot, and stand are also principal design elements. Major points of judging miniature bonsai are discussed below.

The colors of containers should have variety

Miniature bonsai can be exhibited singly, but, because single specimens are inconspicuous, they are often exhibited in groups of five or seven or they are exhibited with one or more companion plantings, such as grasses, bare winter varieties, flowering trees, fruit trees, or red trident maples. To give variety to the display, the sizes of the containers should be of different colors and shapes, but the total effect should be harmonious. In each grouping of miniature bonsai, the colors of the containers should not be repetitive in order to add more variety to the exhibit.

Miniature bonsai should be natural and create an illusion of massiveness

Although miniature bonsai are tiny, their overall shape as composed of roots, trunk, branches, and foliage should correspond to trees found in nature. In the manner of presentation, it is not necessary to be as realistic as when training medium and large bonsai. Using imaginative methods with miniature bonsai will make them more interesting.

A series of plants on display at a miniature bonsai exhibition.

Ceramic containers for miniature bonsai should be rich in color.

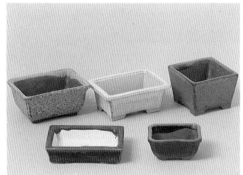

A Japanese flowering quince miniature bonsai.

Harmony, naturalness, and gracefulness should be considered when matching companion or accessory plantings with main exhibits

Evergreens can be displayed with deciduous winter varieties, red trident maples, red mountain maples, flowering varieties, or fruit trees. Trees and grasses of the same geographical region can be displayed together— for instance, alpine trees with alpine grasses, steppe trees with steppe grasses. Stands can be used to regulate the height of exhibits and, when fine rocks and scrolls are added, exhibitions of miniature bonsai can stimulate the viewer's imagination and encourage him to appreciate the infinite delights of nature.

Choosing tree materials

Miniature bonsai materials should have the following characteristics:

Trees that can be easily dwarfed: Because miniature bonsai are small, it is necessary to choose tree materials that are easy to dwarf. In addition, choose trees that send out fine branchlets readily and have small leaves, flowers, and fruit and short internodes.

Trees that do not elongate easily: It is difficult to maintain the shape of a tree that produces long internodes readily; such a tree also tends to lack a feeling of stability.

Trees that can be created into bonsai within a short time: Choose a tree that ages quickly so that its roots, trunk, and branches may acquire an ancient look, or choose one that flowers readily so that the time of creation is reduced.

A Horsetail beefwood miniature bonsai.

The raising of miniature bonsai is easy.

A black pine and an herb miniature bonsai.

A black pine miniature bonsai decoration piece.

Displaying miniature bonsai

Miniature bonsai can be displayed in groups of two, three, five, or seven. Each exhibit should basically be composed of three elements— tree, container, and stand. Companion or accessory plantings should contrast or complement the main exhibits. Furthermore, the size and color of the containers as well as the size and height of the stands should harmonize and unify the composition.

It is best to use trees of different varieties and characteristics as companion plantings. In a bonsai display, avoid including similar varieties and styles in a group. There should be a selection of majestic and delicate trees, refined wind-swept and literati styles, as well as colorful flowering and fruit trees. Try to give the entire arrangement balance and harmony to create a superior visual effect.

The main tree should be placed on the top shelf; it is best to choose one that is aged-looking, strong, or has a driftwood style. As a general rule, the best tree should be centered on the top shelf; but a viewing stone can be used as a substitute. Because the center of the design is the focus of attention, the quality of the tree in the center has considerable influence on the overall design. Grasses and fine rocks can be arranged on lower shelves to make the design more spacious and impart a leisurely feeling.

When displaying miniature bonsai, the focal points of trees on upper and lower shelves should not be in a line, and trees on the sides should not be of the same height or size. Companion plantings on both sides should not be too prominent or placed too high. Finally, the design should correspond to seasonal changes in order to fully represent nature: In spring, flowering trees and trees in bud should be displayed; in summer, trees with lush green foliage create a cool atmosphere; in fall, red-leafed varieties are ideal; and in winter, bare winter trees best match the season Select the trees carefully and arrange them ingeniously to make the whole design lively and pleasing.

PREPARATION FOR BONSAI DISPLAY

The author at the Taipei Fine Arts Museum for a bonsai exhibition.

The plant raised in this ordinary clay pot was very appropriate for growth.

Prior to exhibition, an embellished ceramic container is substituted for the ordinary clay pot to enhance beauty.

Preparation for Bonsai Display

After a long period of watering, fertilizing, trimming, and styling, tree materials eventually become established bonsai. To the bonsai enthusiast, displaying the results of his creative efforts is a happy and momentous occasion. Every enthusiast naturally hopes to exhibit his works in their most beautiful and perfect shapes. Preparation before an exhibition has a direct effort on the viewers' impressions of the bonsai.

Preparation before display

The pot

The pot is one of the three essential elements that constitute a bonsai. To make a good bonsai, all three elements— tree, pot, and soil— must be unified and harmonious. Choosing the pot is very important. When a tree is being trained, it is planted in a large and deep unglazed pot to speed its growth. When it is established, in order to control its overall condition, enhance its beauty, and retain its shape, the bonsai is transplanted into a display or decorative pot. This should be done when the tree is transplanted and repotted in spring.

To fully display the shape of the bonsai and the natural characteristics of the tree species, it is necessary to carefully consider the shape, size, height, and color of the pot as well as the position of the bonsai. For example, old trees should be grown in old pots. After choosing the pot, the bonsai creator should clean its outer surface and beautify it.

Landscaping the soil surface

The color of the soil and the pattern of its surface should match the shape and natural setting of the bonsai. The surface should be uneven and form mounds around the trunk and below thick roots to enhance the illusion that the tree is growing in its natural environment. The viewer can then associate the bonsai with trees growing on hills and plains or by the lakeside. Three or four months before exhibition, moss can be added to the soil surface. Put moss into a tray with water before applying it to the bonsai, clean off unnecessary soil, and plant the moss firmly on the soil surface. Moss is of utmost importance to the overall beauty of the bonsai. It can give a feeling of stability and stop topsoil from being washed away; in a shallow pot containing much soil, it is almost indispensable. Moss should be scattered unevenly over the surface to match the undulating contours of the soil surface, and it should be denser near the base of the tree. Let the roots grow out as naturally as possible. Try to make the design natural; moss should not, however, be too abundant; it should not cover half of the soil surface or it may obstruct the entrance of sunlight and air. Cultivating moss with care underscores the beauty of the bonsai and gives pleasure to the grower and viewer.

Green moss is often used to landscape the soil surface.

The surface soil of a bonsai without green moss is very ordinary in appearance.

The surface soil of the bonsai after the planting of green moss, which imbues the creation with a sense of natural vigor.

A well-chosen container and display stand exhibit an established bonsai to full perfection and beauty.

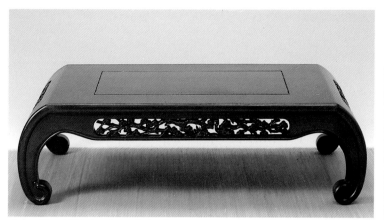

A traditional Chinese bonsai stand.

A Japanese-style bonsai stand.

A traditional Chinese bonsai stand.

The stand

If the pot, tree, and stand are well-matched and complement each other, the artistic effect will be greatly enhanced and the value of the bonsai increased. Stands can be made of wood, bamboo, or natural roots (for indoor displays) and stone or ceramics (for outdoor displays). Stands of various heights and sizes should be chosen to match the species and style of the trees as well as the shape of the pots. There are two types of stands—floor stands and table stands—whose height can be adjusted. In terms of size and height, there are mid-sized stands, regular stands, and wooden stands. In terms of shape, there are round, rectangular, oval, multi-angled, and irregular stands. The surface area of the stand must be slightly greater than that of the pot; round stands are suitable for round pots, quadrilateral stands for quadrilateral or oval pots. As for the shape and line of the stands, powerful and imposing trees like pines and junipers go well with strong and rustic stands; refined and beautiful deciduous varieties go well with delicate stands; group plantings or tray-landscape styles go well with bamboo stands to express a rustic feeling; pots that contribute to overall harmony and unity should be chosen for miniature bonsai. Bonsai with powerful shapes should be placed on stands with thick floors. Delicate bonsai look best on stands with thin floors. Any tree leaning to the left or right should be placed on a rectangular stand to leave space for expansion. Bonsai of poetic design (literati style) should be matched with thin and decorated stands.

A selection of bonsai stands.

A selection of bonsai stands.

A Chinese painting that can be displayed with exhibited bonsai.

艷荷已發賞花人香惟有蜻蜓貪蕙必亦有情妄墨平歲次己巳·韓蝌田漫筆

Backgrounds and companion plantings

In a bonsai exhibition, black can be used as the background color for flowering varieties, fruit trees, and deciduous varieties; for the rest, light gray or ivory is a suitable color. Grasses, scrolls, or fine rocks can be used as accessories to accentuate a feeling either of wildness or refinement. Companion grasses should suit the species of tree; for instance, match alpine grass with alpine trees and steppe grass with steppe trees. Be sure the grass is not too massive or tall or it will become the dominant element in the design. If the soil surface in a bonsai is monotonous and has too much empty space, finely shaped rocks can be added. Pay attention to the amount of empty space in the design and choose rocks of suitable sizes and shapes. It is preferable to choose rocks with deep color because they appear more stable and natural. They should be planted with their bottoms well buried in the soil.

Scrolls can also be displayed at the same time to enhance the feeling of refinement. Companion plantings or ornaments that are perfectly matched with bonsai can heighten the theme and overall effect and engage the imagination of the viewer in the infinite charm of nature created by the whole setting.

Preparing the bonsai

Special care needs to be taken with bonsai before public display. A schedule must be set up and followed to manage the growth of bonsai. Fertilizing the tree to promote vitality and controlling the size of the leaves are important procedures. All wires on the bonsai should be removed. In addition, a little leaf trimming should be done 40 days before and again several days before exhibition to increase the number of fine branchlets. The surface of the trunk and branches must be cleaned. Lime-and-sulphur should be applied repeatedly to jinns and sharies. Before display, trim the leaves and spray leaf surfaces with fertilizers to give the foliage an even and pleasing color.

Herbs can also be used to set off an exhibited bonsai.

Grasses and herbs used to highlight displayed bonsai.

Chinese paintings that can be displayed with exhibited bonsai.

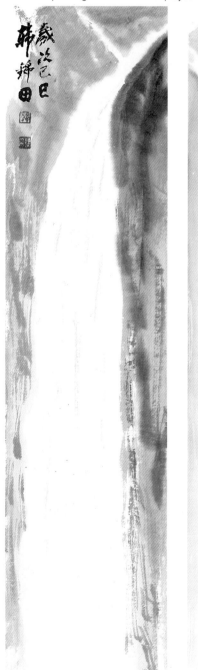

A Chinese painting that can be displayed with exhibited bonsai.

A GUIDE TO BONSAI
APPRECIATION

A beautiful example of a radial root-base.

The beauty of a natural forest is best appreciated from a distance.

A Guide to Bonsai Appreciation

Trees in the wild are viewed from a distance, but bonsai are appreciated at close range. The overall appearance of a bonsai must correspond to the shape and form of the real tree so that the viewer can see what kind of tree it represents; therefore, in the process of creation, it is essential to fully present the characteristics of each species and pay special attention to the details of the root-system, trunk, and branches.

For the best visual effect, the bonsai should be positioned so that the mid-point of the tree is at eye level. This will produce the illusion that the bonsai is massive and that the viewer is looking up at it from ground level.

There are two ways of evaluating bonsai: One is to judge the features of an individual bonsai; the other is to classify bonsai into indoor, outdoor, and exhibition varieties.

Factors in bonsai appreciation

A bonsai may be appreciated through its individual characteristics: roots, stock (lower trunk), trunk, branches, foliage, apex, flowers, fruit, and container.

The roots

The width or extent of the surface roots should be twice the diameter of the stock so that they are in harmony with the tree. The expansion of the surface roots is an important factor in stabilizing the tree; in addition, the branching and thickness of the roots can suggest age in the tree.

There are several types of surface roots, which are classified by the pattern of the root-system:

Radial roots: This is the most ideal pattern. The roots extend outward from the trunk in every direction. Roots on the sides are comparatively longer, while those in front and back are shorter. A radial root-system is best for an upright or coiled style.

One-sided roots: Vigorous roots grow in one single direction or on both sides of the trunk. This type of root-system is most suitable for slanting or cascade styles.

Twisted roots: Established roots become twisted together and form crag-like surface roots. This type of root-system has a feeling of strength and wildness and is used to suggest age in massive trees. Banyans and trident maples usually have these kind of roots.

Exposed roots: Roots are exposed when the surface soil is washed or blown away. This form of root-system is suitable for imitating trees growing in adverse conditions on steep slopes or along rivers and seas.

Roots of young trees grow and differentiate beneath the soil surface. Subjected to sunlight and rain over the years, old roots gradually emerge on the surface. Such roots look aged and twisted and appear to become part of the trunk, balancing and stabilizing the whole tree. Be aware of this natural phenomenon when transplanting a bonsai, and make the soil surface slightly higher than the level of the pot so that part of the root-system is exposed. This creates the feeling that the roots are grasping the soil surface.

The stock

The part of the trunk between the first branch and the root-system is called the stock. The best stock is strong and shaped like a trumpet. The trunk near the roots should be thick and taper gradually to the apex. A good trunk should have elegant lines and curves to give variety to the tree. Because the stock is not covered by foliage or branches, there should be no wounds or scars on the front.

The trunk

The trunk is the most important factor in determining the quality of the entire composition. Single-trunk styles are considered the finest. The trunk must harmonize with the branches and foliage to express the characteristics of the tree species. Pines, trident maples, and Japanese mountain maples have hard and sharp leaves, so the trunk must be delicate and curved. Conversely, Sargent junipers have soft foliage; therefore, the trunk should have strong and well-defined curves.

Necessary characteristics of a good trunk:

(1) The trunk should taper smoothly from a thick base to the apex.

(2) It should be somewhat rounded and without wounds, or it may form an obvious angle with the roots. If the trunk has wounds, should not be positioned in the front.

(3) The trunk should have irregular bends and curves that are natural and smooth in movement. Weathered bark can add a sense of age.

(4) The thickness of the trunk should be in proportion to the height of the tree.

The form or texture of the trunk can be rounded, twisted, gnarled, rough-barked, crackled, jinned, or sharied.

A rounded trunk (Trident maple).

A twisted trunk (Common jasmin orange).

A sharied trunk (Oriental arborvita).

A crackled trunk (Nishiki black pine).

A gnarled trunk (Linden hibiscus).

A rough-barked trunk (Box-tree).

A jinned branch (Needle juniper).

The shape and texture of the trunk have great influence on the overall design; bonsai enthusiasts should, therefore, pay a great deal of attention to the trunk. A good trunk has large and small curves. The following is a list of trunk defects:

S-shaped trunk: The shape of the trunk is a regular "S" shape, which lacks strength and looks unrefined.

Dominant secondary trunk: In a twin-trunk style, the secondary trunk is larger than the main one.

Galled trunk: The middle section of the trunk swells and forms galls or knots. This plant disease is very unsightly.

Recurved trunk: The trunk turns and twists unnaturally, lacking strength and stability.

Frog-legged trunk: In a twin-trunk style, the trunks form an obtuse angle; this is also known as the "surrendering trunk" style.

Pigeon-breasted trunk: The trunk curves like the pigeon's breast and appears weak.

Avoid using tree material with any of these defects.

The branches

The design of the branches should blend with the roots and the trunk. The ideal length of branches is 6 to 8 times the diameter of the trunk. Good branches should have short internodes and dense, fine branchlets. They should also be shaped and arranged in order to display the characteristics of the species. Branches should be thick toward the bottom but thin toward the apex; however, a few thick branches at the top can create a wild and strong effect. For miscellaneous varieties, the branches generally grow upward at an angle of 45 degrees to the trunk, and several branches grow out from one position. As the tree gets older, it stops growing higher. When a bonsai is created, train the branches slightly downward to suggest age.

Based on the species of the bonsai, the ideal shape of the branch may be triangular, oval, elliptical, or semi-circular. The first branch should start about one-third of the way up the trunk. Upper branches should not be of the same length as lower branches. There should be variety in the size and length of the branches to impart a feeling of age. Branches have complicated variations and there are many "do nots" regarding their arrangement. Special attention must be paid to trimming and shaping. Branches in the front should be short and those at the back long; this creates perspective and gives a realistic dimension to the design. The front branches should slant slightly to either the left or the right to avoid creating an oppressive feeling and cluttering up the design. Be sure that branches do not conceal the various features of the trunk and that their starting points are carefully exhibited.

The foliage

Except in deciduous trees during the winter, leaves play an important role in bonsai design. Pay attention to the selection of bonsai materials because the quality of leaves cannot be changed, except through special techniques. Small, neat, simple leaves that show obvious seasonal variations in color are gaining popularity. The proportion of the foliage to roots, trunk, and branches should be agreeable.

The apex

The apex or crown is the uppermost part of the trunk and the point of growth. The size, density, and position of the apex affect the appearance of the bonsai to a large extent. It should lean about 15 degrees to the front so that the viewer seems to be looking up from ground level at a lofty and massive tree.

The flowers

The most colorful part of the plant is the flower. Different flowers have different implications. In feasts or celebrations, flowering bonsai help create a festive atmosphere. The size of the flowers should be in proportion to that of the tree; otherwise, even the best flowering variety will lose its appeal. Preferably, the tree should have a long florescence and the flowers open fully when it blossoms; the flowers should also be bright-colored and show variation.

The fruit

Fruit represents the renewal of life and is the result of great effort. Fruiting bonsai are very appealing to people and play important roles in miniature bonsai. After the tree flowers, its fruit begins to grow. The fruit should be in proportion to the tree. It may stay on the tree for quite a long time. The tree should have a heavy crop of fruit that shows variation in color. It is also enjoyable to grow some eatable fruit.

The pot

Judging a container or pot depends mainly on whether it harmonizes with the tree and contributes to the beauty of the overall design. Thus, it is necessary to choose pots of different colors, shapes, sizes, and textures to match and complement the species, styles, ages, and characteristics of the trees.

A beautiful natural tree with a rich profusion of trunk tumors.

An extremely dense treetop presents the full beauty of a natural tree.

A root-over-rock trident maple adorning a window frame.

Indoor display

In places where walls are light in color or where there is a lot of empty space—for example, in a hallway or living room or on a mantelpiece or low table—appealing bonsai can be highlighted with spotlights. There are many points to be considered in the display of bonsai.

The stand or table

Choose display stands or tables of various shapes, textures, sizes, and colors that correspond to the tree species. For instance, flowering and fruiting varieties, miscellaneous varieties, grass, and young bonsai with slender trunks can be displayed on stands made of red sandalwood, Chinese quince, bamboo, or natural roots. For strong species like pines and junipers, hard and rustic stands of red sandalwood or Chinese quince should be chosen. The shapes of stands can be square, round, or rectangular. There are both floor and table stands, which should be chosen to match the style of the bonsai.

Positioning the bonsai

Large and medium bonsai: These should be displayed in spacious areas. If a tree leans to the left, it should be placed to the right of the stand; ornamental grass may then be placed to the left and slightly to the front. This arrangement creates a feeling of harmony and balance. At banquets or parties, pines and junipers can be displayed as the main exhibits, with miscellaneous varieties as companion plantings, and decorative grass, bamboo, or fine rocks placed in the middle of the design.

A medium-size Fukien tea bonsai on a stand set in front of a wall for appreciation.

A clean and magnificent Japanese grey-bark elm bonsai used as interior decoration.

Bonsai arranged on outdoor shelves for appreciation.

Bonsai on a platform decorates the corner of a garden.

Miniature bonsai: These plants should be displayed on stands of various shapes and sizes to enhance their daintiness and delicacy.

Rock plantings: These should be displayed with grass on stands or tables. Generally, it is best to use small, soft grasses as companion plantings. Companion plantings should not be too conspicuous or they will detract from the beauty of the rock plantings.

Weeping styles: Full cascades and semi-cascades should be displayed on high stands with their branches flowing downward. Placing grass or rocks at the foot of the stands will add to the elegance and refinement of the exhibit.

If bonsai are displayed indoors, they should be placed so that the midpoint of each tree is at eye level when the viewer is standing. If bonsai are placed on desks, wine cabinets, or long stands, the viewer should be able to appreciate them at eye level when he is sitting.

When displaying bonsai indoors, keep in mind that bonsai cannot be kept inside for more than three days and that they require frequent leaf spraying. They should not be kept in an air-conditioned or heated room for more than one day, lest the trees suffer dehydration due to rapid evaporation. More attention should also be paid to trees during hot summer and when they are in bud.

Outdoor display

In the courtyard or on the balcony, bonsai can be placed on wooden or concrete shelves. When displayed on shelves, larger bonsai should be placed in back and smaller ones in front. The arrangement should not be too orderly. There should be different heights and sizes of trees to create perspective and depth; for example, fine rocks or grasses can be displayed as companion plants beside pines, red trident maples, Japanese mountain maples, bare winter trees, flowering varieties, and fruit trees. Miniature bonsai or rocks placed on ceramic trays are also suitable companions. Lights can be installed if you want to enjoy bonsai at night with your family or friends.

INDEX